W9-BOK-387

Sharing a
PLACE
Without Losing Your
SPACE

A COUPLE'S GUIDE TO BLENDING HOMES, LIVES, AND CLUTTER

Sharing a
PLACE
Without Losing Your
SPACE

A COUPLE'S GUIDE TO BLENDING HOMES, LIVES, AND CLUTTER

Regina Leeds

ALPHA

A member of Penguin Group (USA) Inc.

Copyright © 2003 by Regina Leeds

All rights reserved. No part of this book shall be reproduced, stored in a retrieval system, or transmitted by any means, electronic, mechanical, photocopying, recording, or otherwise, without written permission from the publisher. No patent liability is assumed with respect to the use of the information contained herein. Although every precaution has been taken in the preparation of this book, the publisher and author assume no responsibility for errors or omissions. Neither is any liability assumed for damages resulting from the use of information contained herein. For information, address Alpha Books, 201 West 103rd Street, Indianapolis, IN 46290.

International Standard Book Number: 1-59257-060-7
Library of Congress Catalog Card Number: 2003104301

05   04   03   8   7   6   5   4   3   2   1

Interpretation of the printing code: The rightmost number of the first series of numbers is the year of the book's printing; the rightmost number of the second series of numbers is the number of the book's printing. For example, a printing code of 03-1 shows that the first printing occurred in 2003.

Printed in the United States of America

Note: This publication contains the opinions and ideas of its author. It is intended to provide helpful and informative material on the subject matter covered. It is sold with the understanding that the author and publisher are not engaged in rendering professional services in the book. If the reader requires personal assistance or advice, a competent professional should be consulted.

The author and publisher specifically disclaim any responsibility for any liability, loss, or risk, personal or otherwise, which is incurred as a consequence, directly or indirectly, of the use and application of any of the contents of this book.

Trademarks: All terms mentioned in this book that are known to be or are suspected of being trademarks or service marks have been appropriately capitalized. Alpha Books and Penguin Group (USA) Inc. cannot attest to the accuracy of this information. Use of a term in this book should not be regarded as affecting the validity of any trademark or service mark.

Most Alpha books are available at special quantity discounts for bulk purchases for sales promotions, premiums, fund-raising, or educational use. Special books, or book excerpts, can also be created to fit specific needs.

For details, write: Special Markets, Alpha Books, 375 Hudson Street, New York, NY 10014.

This book is dedicated to the healers and friends who guided me through the personal challenges of 2002. Their love and assistance made the writing of this book not only possible but a joy. I am forever in their debt.

CONTENTS

1 Who's Going to Solve This? .1

2 The Story of Your "Stuff" .23

3 *Moving* Doesn't Have to Be a Dirty Word! 57

4 The Bedrooms 79

5 The Kitchen 105

6 The Bathrooms and Linen Closet 133

7 The Common Rooms 149

8 The Children's Rooms and Guest Room 165

9 The Garage, Attic, and Storage Units 181

10 The Home Office 195

11 Creating a Sacred Space 219

Resources 237

Index 241

INTRODUCTION

It begins while we are in-utero. Some well-meaning person hosts a baby shower in our honor and, by the time we're born, we are officially members of the human race: We've got "stuff"! If you are the first child, your stuff will be merging into the existing household of your parents. If siblings are present, the merge is more complicated. Not only will physical possessions be moved into new locations, seismic shifts in the emotional lives of all household members also take place. It's a harbinger of things to come: sleepovers, college dorms, first apartments, marriage, moves to the homes of our children, retirement communities. The list is endless!

We spend a good part of our lives learning how to share an environment. The problems that we encounter generally have a lack of organizing skills at their heart. This book offers solid how-to techniques that will enable you to merge your possessions with other human beings in a thoughtful and efficient manner. Blending households needn't be a battleground for unfinished emotional baggage. Indeed, this continuing life challenge can be viewed as a creative adventure. One's physical space should not be the focal point of any emotional challenges that arise as households are merged. Rather, the space should be empowered as a source of support. Home is meant to be a sanctuary, not a war zone.

When I was a little girl growing up in Brooklyn, New York, my mother could have been the poster child for "Overprotective Mothers of America." I clearly remember one Sunday asking for permission to go to the park with my best friend and his family. Our outing was to include going out on the small Prospect Park lake in a rowboat. My mother refused. She was sure the boat would capsize and I would drown. What can I say? Her intentions were good, albeit a bit suffocating at times!

My baby doctor took care of children up to the age of 16. Sainted Dr. Nichols was never once put off or cowed by my mother's overprotective, fear-based behavior. Every time I had to get a shot, for instance, the same drama played itself out. Mom would drive herself into the far corner of the office, wailing a plaintive mantra that went something like this: "Oh! My God! My baby! Oh! My baby is getting a shot!" I would become transfixed by my mother's odd behavior. Children think of their parents as fearless. My strong, powerful mother seemed reduced to Jell-O by the prospect of my receiving a shot. Should *I* be afraid?

Dr. Nichols never missed a beat. He would look at my mom and smile. Then he would turn to me and say gently, "Look at your mother, Regina! Isn't she acting silly? Now, I don't want you to look at her. I want you to watch what I am doing. People are only afraid of what they do not understand." He would painstakingly explain that the shot would not hurt me if I did three things: notice how tightly he was holding my arm, take note of the alcohol swab and the pressure he used in applying it, and finally, watch the shot being administered. Dr. Nichols never failed me. The shots never hurt. And therein lies the moral to the tale: The more you understand something, the less likely you are to be hurt or frightened by it. In this book, I'll show you how you can apply this principle to the task of merging households.

ACKNOWLEDGMENTS

This book was the brainchild of Alpha Books senior acquisitions editor Mike Sanders. I want to thank him for seeing the possibilities after reading the section on merging households in our first collaboration, *The Zen of Organizing.*

Marilyn Allen is the literary agent you dream about. She is a kind, hardworking, gentle woman who has always understood my work and encouraged me as a writer. I want to especially thank her for opening the door at Alpha Books for me.

Bob Diforio is also my agent. He negotiated my contract right after another deal fell through. Bob's patience with me this year has been monumental. I hope he knows how grateful I am.

Lynn Northrup worked with me as my editor. Lynn molded the original manuscript in a loving and gentle way. Most amazing of all, she did her work without ever once tampering with my voice or my message. I am forever in her debt.

Special kudos to everyone at Alpha Books whose creative hands touched the original manuscript. Friends who knew I had originally self-published *The Zen of Organizing* asked if I minded "losing control" of the manuscript. I laughed and assured everyone that it takes a village to birth a book. My village happens to be populated by creative angels!

Ernie and Patty Weckbaugh guided me through the process of self-publishing and did the original illustrations for *The Zen of Organizing* when it was picked up by Alpha Books in the summer of 2000. Ernie was kind enough to supply the illustrations you see in this book. Ernie and Patty work harder than anyone I know. They became more than my collaborators. They are a part of my extended family.

We all have years we love and those we can't wait to see come to an end. I would not have survived the emotional roller coaster of 2002 without the love and assistance of my family of friends and healers. When the time is appropriate, I hope to tell the story of this year. Like most writers, long before the first word is written, I know the title: *Don't Fall Off the Dance Floor!*

I have been blessed to have a best friend who works with me. I can turn on a computer. I can create a document in Word. I can surf the web. And that is the extent of my technological talent! Without Susie Ribnik to desktop-publish each chapter before it was sent to Lynn Northrup, I would have been lost. Susie is the only person outside of Alpha Books who reads my work in progress. I trust her judgment and rely on her honesty. I also wish to thank Susie for her patience with me. She knows the cranky side of the "zen organizer" and loves me in spite of myself!

Every writer relies on his muse. Mine happens to be Katie, the world's greatest Golden Retriever. Katie sat with me during the writing of *The Zen of Organizing*. When that project ended, she abandoned my office. I thought her companionship during that book was a fluke. But the minute I began this book, Miss Katie was once again by my side. Our family grew this year and Katie has been most patient. Murphy, the world's crankiest cockatiel, joined us. Murphy sat in his cage during the writing phase. He sat on my head during rewrites. I have no doubt that this is significant.

1

WHO'S GOING
TO SOLVE THIS?

*"It is impossible to get out of a
problem using the same kind
of thinking that it took to get
into the problem."*

—*Albert Einstein*

People frequently ask me to tackle problems in their environments
without being conscious that the underlying issue in the scenario
they are describing has nothing to do with the world of getting
organized. Here are a few sample questions I have been asked at
seminars that fall into this category:

◆ My spouse is a packrat (or perfectionist, procrastinator, etc.).
  How can I get him/her to change his/her behavior?

◆ My children refuse to help around the house no matter what
  I do. How do you get children to participate?

◆ My spouse says that housework is "women's work" and will
  not lift a finger around the house. How can I get him to help
  out?

◆ I admit I'm a packrat (or perfectionist, procrastinator, etc.). What's wrong with that?

Many of you may read these questions and identify with the issues. They are garden variety in most homes. Here are the questions I ask in return:

◆ Did you notice before you got married that your spouse was a packrat (or procrastinator, perfectionist, etc.) or is this new behavior? Nine times out of ten, the behavior was present and a presumption was made: The "bliss" of living together would automatically result in the desired behavioral change.

◆ At what point in time did you teach your children that helping out around the house was an elective activity, or worse, that you deserved no help and/or respect for the contribution you make as the mother in the home? Children learn to help around the house in much the same way they learn to say "please" and "thank you"—repetition, rewards, and consequences.

◆ I can only presume that a man who describes housework as "women's work" either has a warped sense of humor or is a dyed in the wool misogynist. There had to be other clues.

◆ If you are the packrat/perfectionist/procrastinator, have you ever noticed how much control you exert over the household by your unwillingness to behave in a way that does not drive the other members of your household right up the wall?

Do you catch my drift here? There are two phases to this. The key first phase is to uncover the hidden, or at least unacknowledged, emotional relationships we have to the physical stuff in our lives. Second, we need to put in place a practical plan to set up and organize a home. Blending households is admittedly a huge task. Love and respect for your partner will help you weather any storms you may encounter.

Take heart! There are charts, diagrams, and lists throughout this book to help you. I'll give you step-by-step instructions for every phase of your merge, from the actual move to the details of organizing those pesky tasks like setting up the DVD collection.

Along with the practical information, however, will be material designed to help you uncover some of the emotional issues driving the physical challenges you may be experiencing as you seek to establish your new home. If you aren't the kind of person who can fathom writing in a journal, see if taking a few minutes a day to contemplate the questions posed here helps you gain understanding. It's amazing what you can accomplish over a cup of coffee while the rest of the world thinks you're daydreaming!

If you force a change to your current "way of being" to suit your new situation, you are almost surely doomed to fall back into old habits. Those habits are ingrained in your psyche as "the way things are done." The new behavior is apt to feel strange and imposed. Journal work can help uncover the seeds of the current behavior as they were sown in your past. This knowledge will give you a strong base from which to launch a new life in a new household.

Let me start by introducing you to a lady I met at a social function. Her story struck a chord with me. I hope it will help you as well.

FIRESTORM OF CHANGE

"Lucy," as we'll call her, was a very successful businesswoman. We met at a social function sponsored by one of her clients. I was there to answer "space challenges" from an organizing point of view. My feng shui master was there to offer more esoteric ways of dealing with the situation. Lucy said she had long ago stopped trying to toss things she no longer needed. "No sooner do I toss something," she said, "then I find I need it within a short space of time. What do you think about that?" she asked almost defiantly. Her two cohorts nodded in agreement. This obviously happened to them as well.

I wondered aloud what had happened to Lucy in her past that would have caused this "consciousness of loss" to take hold in her life. This is one of the most common fears active in my clients' lives. It manifests in many ways. Lucy could not give away any possessions for fear they would soon be needed. You'd have to live in a home the size of Buckingham Palace to house the "stuff" of a lifetime and never release any of it!

For other clients, paper takes on a magical significance. Magazines and newspapers pile to the ceiling because someone is convinced that an article they "need" is in the stack. They have no clue what the article might be about but they sense its magical presence in the pile. Every piece of mail that enters the house is treasured. Ancient tax papers the IRS wouldn't have the time to research are stashed into attics, behind doors and into garages that no longer house automobiles due to the crush of papers.

Lucy assured me that absolutely nothing was at work here from the past. I told her that I never force clients to do anything that makes them feel the least bit uncomfortable. If she wanted to save everything, it was her right. My hunch was that her belief that she would shortly need whatever she had tossed would absolutely become her reality. This is called a "consciousness of loss." It becomes a self-fulfilling prophesy. Who was I to rob her of that security? Lucy and her friends relaxed.

As we began to exchange small talk, I encouraged Lucy to tell me about herself. Lo and behold, a powerful experience revealed itself. It seemed that when Lucy was about five years old, she went on her first sleepover to a friend's house. When she returned the next morning, a terrible accident had happened. Her family home had been burned to the ground. Lucy had not only lost everything, she had not had time to take anything that was sacred to her. It would be devastating for a 40-year-old to return home and find that everything he or she owned had gone up in smoke. For a child, I could only assume the trauma would be even greater. I suggested to Lucy that this seminal experience was the genesis of her consciousness of loss. This intellectual revelation might free her from her attachment. It would more likely need to be associated with some short-term therapy. The choice would be hers. Sometimes we become so attached to our neuroses, fears, and fetters, we do not wish to release them.

WHAT'S HIDDEN IN YOUR PAST?

Throughout this book you'll find lists of questions that appear in shaded boxes. These are questions that you'll answer in a special notebook designated for this purpose only. I'll talk more about this in a moment. For now, here are a few sample questions based on Lucy's experience. They are designed to get you thinking in a creative way about your past:

◆ Can you relate to Lucy's story? If so, how?

◆ Is there a fear operating in your life that exerts an adverse affect on your environment?

◆ Do any behaviors manifest from this fear that make life more difficult in your home?

◆ How difficult would it be for you to contemplate change in this area?

◆ Is there any possibility that on some level (perhaps as yet unacknowledged) you enjoy the manifestation of fear? Does it make you feel more powerful?

The last question may strike you as odd. Ironically, the very things that cause us pain or anxiety can sometimes make us feel unique or special. They can draw attention to us in a way that we are attached to and have no idea how to replace. To illustrate, let me tell you about Marilyn.

I'M LATE! I'M LATE! FOR A VERY IMPORTANT DATE ...!

Many years ago I was invited to a private spa and asked to give a talk on the spiritual aspects of getting organized. One of the women in my audience captivated my heart instantly. Marilyn was young, pretty, and five months pregnant. She glowed with the happiness of someone about to bring a new life into the world. She not only laughed easily, her laughter was infectious. Marilyn was there with her best friend—a last time for them to be away from their husbands before the years of babies and small children made their demands. It was a delight to have her in my class.

At the end of my talk, I opened up the room for questions. I was astonished to hear that Marilyn was concerned about her ability to be a good mother. She said she had absolutely no sense of time. How would she get her child ready for school? How would she cope with the additional children she hoped to have with her husband? I was astonished because my perception of Marilyn was that she was very "together." The telltale signs were there. She dressed with great care. Her grooming was impeccable. She had certainly arrived on time for class! Here again, I silently wondered about her past. I asked her how long she had had problems with time.

With absolutely no hesitation, anecdote after anecdote about her never-ending problems with the concept of time came pouring out of Marilyn. The stories were not remarkable in any way. What was completely remarkable was the unrecognized glee she had in recounting them to us. It was clear that from the time she was a young teenager controlling time made Marilyn the star of the show. Friends honked their car horns when she was late for a party. Dates languished in the living room with her parents while she agonized over the final details of her outfit. Everyone waited for Marilyn!

She was not afraid she would not be a good mother. I rather felt she was afraid to give up her star status! I shared my hunch gently with Marilyn. The class gasped. Marilyn was stunned for about 20 seconds. And then a small smile crossed her face and she said sheepishly, "I think you're right!" I have no doubt that all these many years later Marilyn has grown into a wonderful mother whose many accomplishments continue to make her the star of the show!

THE HEALING JOURNAL

When I was a little girl growing up an only child in Brooklyn, I kept a diary. I can see it to this day. It was soft pink and baby blue. The cover had a girl with a ponytail on it just like me. Like all little girls, I needed a safe place to record my innermost thoughts and dreams. My father was in many ways a remarkable man. I hope you will come to know him in the pages of this book. He kept a diary. In fact, he encouraged me to have one. He said it was important at the end of every day to have something significant to record. He told me he didn't want my life to pass without my making some contribution to humanity.

I hope you will consider keeping a diary (nowadays we call them journals) during the process of reading this book. I confess I have become a total "cyber child" and love to write at the computer. My daily journal entries are therefore recorded in a "folder" on my hard drive. Ironically, I also have special hardcopy journals that I frequently travel with. Each is dedicated to one of the books I plan to write in the future. Sometimes I grab one and go to the local coffeehouse and while away a few hours working on some future project that seems to be streaming into my consciousness at that moment in time. I am careful to match the color and design of the journal to aspects of the project.

The bottom line here is that your journal should be perfectly matched to suit your personality. You want this to be an inviting, enriching, and emotionally nurturing experience. This isn't meant to be a homework assignment. Your journal should also be private! Please keep it tucked away from prying eyes. You don't want to find yourself having to explain some things you feel free to express in writing to anyone who might be hurt by your words.

Try and limit your time. I would say that two minutes of immediate "stream of consciousness" replies for each question posed in this book would most likely produce valuable material. I am not interested in exquisite penmanship, perfect grammar, or the "right" responses. And you shouldn't be, either! We are in quest of the truth. We want to uncover any information that can help us make today easier. The environments we create are physical manifestations of our primary thought patterns and belief systems. Later in the day, if time permits, you can expound on your discoveries. We can all find creative ways to short circuit the healing journey. Taking time from daily obligations to family, friends, and work because you have to write in your journal is not what we're after here.

CHOOSING A JOURNAL

Although any spiral-bound notebook will do, if possible, purchase a special journal for your journey through this book. There are many lovely designs available in stores. If you prefer, record your journal entries on your computer.

After selecting your journal and designating a set time each day to do your exercises, please take approximately 15 minutes to answer the following questions (just skip the ones that don't relate to your situation).

1. What attracted you to this book? What do you hope to learn from it?

2. Do you have a habit that drives your spouse/children/parents up the wall?

3. Are you willing to try and change this habit? Have you ever tried to address your issues before? What were the results?

4. Why would this attempt be different for you?

5. On the other hand, is there something about a person in your environment that makes you crazy? Can you be specific? (This person is lazy, a perfectionist, procrastinator, etc.)

6. Is this person aware of his/her behavior? Have you discussed it previously? What happened?

Now please take 10 minutes to respond in your journal to the following 5 questions listed after the story of Lucy.

1. Did you relate to Lucy's story? If so, how?
2. Is there a fear operating in your life that exerts an adverse affect on your environment?
3. Do any behaviors manifest from this fear that make life more difficult in your home?
4. How difficult would it be for you to contemplate change in this area?
5. Is there any possibility that on some level (perhaps as yet unacknowledged) you enjoy the manifestation of fear? Does it make you feel more powerful?

THE INNER TEACHER

A little more than 20 years ago, when I was first blessed to discover self-help books, I never bothered to do any of the journal work that was almost universally suggested. What would be the point? After all, I knew what the answers would be. Why take the time to stop and write? I was in a hurry for the "cure." I needed to keep reading!

Then a miracle happened. I had read John Bradshaw's books, *Healing the Shame That Binds* and *The Family.* I was ready to tackle his third book, *Homecoming,* and follow John's ground-breaking work on the inner child. The latter is filled with important exercises. For the first time in my life, I picked up a pen and paper. I was amazed. The process of writing and the process of intellectually responding to questions were indeed not the same. What tumbled out of me floored me. At last I had some of the necessary keys to unlock the chains of the past. I can't promise you'll have the same experience. I can suggest, however, that similar revelations may be waiting for you, if you are open to the experience. Please do whatever feels right for you at this time.

ARE YOU TALKIN' TO ME?

I grew up in Brooklyn at a time when no one was questing for his inner child, reading self-help books, talking about spiritual philosophy, or espousing the virtues of 12-step programs. As Catholics in the 1950s and 1960s, we were urged, in fact, to bring all of our woes to the priest in the confessional. Therapy was for crazy people. The big message was don't rock the boat!

My parents were not prepared for a child who would take delight in rocking the boat! I think they spent most of their lives scratching their heads in wonder as they tried to figure out this child they loved so much. I am old enough now to look back and see the thread that brought me to the place I am now. In a sense, I was born to organize people and write about it. I was also one of the last people to figure that out.

My first love was acting. I wanted to make people laugh the way Lucy, Uncle Miltie, and Sid Caesar did. The culture in Brooklyn at that time was primarily European immigrant. A strong work ethic infused every aspect of my life. I transferred that love of excellence to my study of acting. Why bother if you weren't driven to be the best? Success in show business is not, I was to discover, commensurate with the purity of your intentions or the excellence of your studies.

During the year of my greatest success as an actress, when I had a recurring role on *The Young and the Restless* and appeared in several national commercials, I took stock of my life. I wanted some security. These were fun but I feared ultimately dead-end assignments. The struggle inherent in an actor's life is only romantic when you are young. I had to come to grips with the fact that the crapshoot called "acting" might not end in the way I had dreamed. My organizing business began in secret. Almost ten years later, I walked away from acting, embraced my organizing business full time, and wrote my first book, *The Zen of Organizing: Creating Order and Peace in Your Home, Career, and Life* (see the appendix at the end of this book for details). The rest, as they say, is history!

In an ironic twist of fate, acting serves me well to this day. As a seminar leader and teacher, I never suffer stage fright. I am amused to remember notes sent home over the years from teachers urging my parents to encourage me to write for a living. I am grateful I overcame my fears and confronted myself in therapy. I remember with great amusement how organized my mother was and how her philosophy has shaped what I teach. And more than anything else, I am thankful my creative nature led me to a study of Eastern spiritual philosophy. These seemingly unrelated interests and activities brought me to a place where I could in fact help others. The journey I had planned was not nearly as exquisite as the one I discovered.

I can hear some of you asking: "Are you talkin' to me?" I have told you something about myself for one very important reason. You and I are going to be taking something of an adventure together. I think it's nice to know the tour guide, don't you? I wanted to be sure you knew that not only was I talking to you, I had already walked the walk that accompanied the talk!

HOME AS SANCTUARY

If you are about to embark on a shared life with another human being, I hope it will be an opportunity for you to discover yourselves and explore new options. Home is the place you should enter at day's end to be nurtured. This belief is the touchstone of my work as a professional organizer. Home is where you will want to feel safe and replenish your soul. It is too often a war zone of unresolved emotional issues and chaos.

Are you willing to play a little game with me? Let's consider for a minute one of the ways we learn things about other people. In the entertainment industry, they have artisans known as set decorators. The writer's material needs to be turned into a set. This is what you see as an audience when the curtain rises in the theater or when the house lights go down in the movie theater. Turn on the TV right now and search for a show you have never seen before. What does the physical environment tell you about the people living there? Are they middle class, poor, or well-to-do? Are they sloppy or prissy? Do you see evidence of any hobbies? Do they like to read? Are there antiques everywhere or is modern taste what rules? Try this for a minute.

Our homes so exquisitely express our emotions that we rarely take the time to see them as others do. It's as if we decorate them while we are unconscious! I am always amazed, for instance, by my clients' ability to quite literally hide who they are. I helped organize a wonderful attorney a few years ago who lived in a duplex. The upstairs told you volumes about Roy. I knew his spiritual affiliation, his profession, his hobbies, and the fact that he was in a relationship instantly. The downstairs, however, was a vast wasteland. Every interesting facet of Roy's personality was kept hidden. The walls were bare. The furniture and the carpet were lifeless, utilitarian. It was as if you might enter his living space but you had to be invited into the upstairs inner sanctum before you could get to really know him!

Roy was shocked when I pointed this out to him. We had a wonderful time sifting through his possessions, deciding what would be shared with family and friends. A few colorful pillows and a throw for the couch and the entire feel of the home had changed. We added a small rug under the coffee table, hung some of his artwork and displayed a few souvenirs from his many world travels. The change was remarkable. Here's an exercise for you to do and, if you feel comfortable, remember you can record your responses in your journal.

Please exit your home or apartment. Prepare to walk through as if you have never been here before nor do you know any of the occupants. Walk slowly from room to room. Now please take a minute to answer the following questions in your journal.

1. What is your immediate impression of the person who lives here? (For example: Do you think they have lived here a long time or does the sight of many boxes lead you to believe they may have just moved in?)

2. Can you list 5 to 10 things about the resident that is revealed by the physical environment? (I have a Golden Retriever and my couch is always covered for her convenience. In addition, the floor is littered with dog toys. In much the same way, a home with children will frequently have toys scattered about or you'll see school papers on the kitchen counter.)

3. What 5 to 10 things do you feel the resident could do immediately to make the space more inviting? Make a list. (This might be something like seeing the need for a bigger coffee table in the family room or it could be as simple as noticing an overflowing hamper and make a note to do the laundry!)

4. Take about five minutes to express your overall feelings about this exercise. What have you discovered?

Think this sounds silly and you can't do it? You already have many times. How? Every time we find out that *unexpected* company is coming over, we do a variation on this exercise. Haven't you ever thrown out a stack of newspapers from the den because your relatives are popping by and you suddenly see how unsightly it is? Have you ever madly tossed a pile of things stacked on your bed into a closet because you don't want your mother or best friend to make a comment about your messy bedroom? You get the idea. Have fun with this exercise.

THE URGE TO MERGE

If you and your partner are preparing to merge households and the move has not yet taken place, please do the previous exercise the next time you go to your future mate's current dwelling. But be discreet. I would feel judged or violated if someone I loved announced that he was now doing an exercise to determine the state of my home. Why not casually do the walk-through while he or she is in the shower? You can record your responses when you get home.

Here are two additional questions to answer in your journal.

1. What 5 to 10 things do you see here that would drive you up the wall if you had to live with them? Make a list. Remember, we don't magically change just because we are now sharing an environment. Love is the most powerful force in the universe. If your future spouse is a packrat today, he or she may worship the ground you glide over, but they are most likely still going to be a packrat after you move in. Love won't change that aspect of their personality.

2. As you look at your list, are some of the current conditions easily remedied? For example, you may now realize that your beloved hates to do laundry and puts it off until every last article of clothing, sheet, and towel is dirty. You on the other hand may love doing the laundry (I do!) and this would pose no problem.

Other items on your list may take some negotiating to work out a system before you move in. For example, if your intended never lifts a finger in the home and has not yet been introduced to everyday appliances like the vacuum cleaner, can you afford to have some cleaning assistance in the home? If not, will you be resentful that maintenance of the home is now your responsibility? Better to figure these things out now.

I wouldn't necessarily talk about the exercise in this way: "Say, I did what professional organizer Regina Leeds suggested and now I realize that you are a slob. Are you willing to work out a housekeeping system before we move in?" By the time you peel your partner off the wall, any chance of successful negotiating will have been lost.

I once dated a guy who threw his dirty clothes on the floor, made the bed only when the Board of Health called, and let every dish he owned pile up to the ceiling before he would start washing the stack. Needless to say, it gave me pause. I guessed his background was the culprit. He was the youngest in a large family of girls. He grew up with caretakers. I asked him one day if his background had been a contributing factor in making him untidy. Had the women in his family doted on him by doing all the chores, and unwittingly "crippled" him? He said he hadn't thought about it and wondered where the question came from. I pointed out his inability to wash dishes, change sheets, or clean clothes until every last resource had been exhausted. He was stunned. It had not occurred to him. We negotiated a successful division of tasks.

Remember, too, that you can only change yourself. Trying to change another human being is folly. The most powerful way to positively influence another human being is by being an example of the behavior you wish to experience in return. When women ask me how to motivate their husbands and children, I suggest they start to get organized first. Unless there is severe dysfunction in the family unit, everyone is going to notice that something is happening with Mom. Organization brings order and that in turn allows peace to settle over the home. Everyone will be encouraged to get into the act and participate.

IT BEARS REPEATING ...

Psychologists say it takes 21 *consecutive* days of repeating an action before it becomes a habit. You'd be surprised how even the tiniest action can have a huge impact on your environment!

If your home is a hotbed of chaos, the best way to start to change yourself (and the environment in the process) is by establishing good habits. Here are my favorite good habits to establish. See if any of these feel right as a place for you to start your personal transformation:

◆ Make the bed every day.

◆ Don't leave dirty dishes in the sink. Wash them immediately.

◆ Put the clean dishes away rather than letting them languish on the drain board after they've dried.

◆ Put your keys in the same place every time you enter your home.

◆ Take the garbage out every day.

Can you think of five additional habits you would like to establish? Please note your list in your journal so you won't forget! If this seems overwhelming to you, remember that we do things by rote all the time. Would you leave the house without brushing your teeth? Do you ever not comb your hair and enter the world with "bed head"? You see what I mean? All we are doing is adding to our list of automatic good habits that make life easier.

Be sure you pick *repeatable actions* than can become automatic. A client once called me and proudly announced that the good habit she was establishing was working on cleaning out her files. This is an example of a *project,* not a repeatable *action.* Be sure you pick things that fall into the latter category. Keep them simple, and don't tackle too many all at once. Three new habits at one time is a good limit.

BUT MY MOTHER DID IT THIS WAY!

Several years ago I met a man who was strongly enmeshed in the patterns of the past. They brought him security. Now although I certainly believe that honoring tradition is a wonderful thing, it can work against us when the traditions of our youth box us into a prison. For example, Bob always had to have Sunday dinner at the same time. He always ushered guests to the table the minute they entered the home. The menu for special occasions could not vary. His wife, who had been raised in a completely different ethnic background, was driven nuts by all the rules and regulations.

Do you relate to Bob? Perhaps when you made the list in your journal of the things that would drive you crazy, your list was unconsciously based on the "but my mother always did it this way" mentality. Let me tell you how I broke free of this pattern. I grew up with a mother who was the most fastidious housekeeper you could imagine. Eating off the floors was a viable option. I grew up copying my mother's routine. One of the "rules" in the home was that the ever-perfect state of the coffee table had to be maintained. Nothing was to be tossed in a haphazard manner on its surface. Every item was chosen carefully and placed just so.

Flash forward in time. I am an adult living across the country in California. Needless to say, I have a perfect coffee table display at all times. Magazines are always up to date and edge to edge, flowers are fresh, knick-knacks are placed with the precision of a drill team. In short, the display is perfect!

One day a dear friend flew to Los Angeles from New York for a visit. As it happens, she had a serious illness. We never knew what visit would be our last. On her last evening with me, while she was in the guest bathroom, I noticed that the order of the coffee table had to be restored. I was annoyed. How could she not see how awful it looked? Why hadn't she returned items to their original locations? Why weren't the magazines edge to edge? It took only a minute for me to "fix" it.

When my friend returned to the living room, she saw immediately what I had done. She never said a word. I saw the expression on her face. In an instant, I understood that she felt judged. I had wanted her to respect the perfect environment I had created. I had instead treated her like a child. I realized in a flash how anal and absurd it was to adjust the coffee table while we were in that room enjoying it. I never did anything like that again. I still restore my coffee table. I just don't do it during a visit or a party. I have more respect for others now.

Many of us grow up thinking that the way we have done things is the way they should continue to be done. Why not open yourself to other possibilities? Maybe hidden in that list of things that drive you crazy is the key to a new freedom. Before we move on to the next chapter, spend a few minutes with your list. Here are some questions to help guide your exploration of "Momma's way of doin' things."

1. Why would a change in the way something is done be so difficult for you?
2. What feelings do you have attached to this activity?
3. Is there a possibility that this activity is a veiled attempt to help you control the new environment and, in effect, your partner?
4. Please write for about five minutes expressing how this last exercise has made you feel. Are you delighted that new opportunities are at hand? Or are you uncomfortable and full of fear?

CHARTING YOUR PATH

As I've shared, my mother was a fastidious housekeeper. She had a set day for every major task in the home. Unless there was a major rain or snowstorm in Brooklyn, my mother would be washing the windows of our brownstone on the same day each week. Many of you probably have similar routines for keeping your home tidy and organized. For those of you who have no idea how to run a household, here is a basic chart to get you started.

Fill in the blanks as they relate to your living situation. A one-bedroom apartment, for instance, is easier to maintain than a one-bedroom house with a porch and a backyard. A house with no pets tends to stay in pristine condition longer than one with a dog or a cat. (As the "human mother" of a Golden Retriever and a very messy cockatiel, I can assure you, the emotional rewards are well worth the mess!)

You can shape this chart to suit your needs. You might want to use this chart but continue to shift responsibilities as children grow and become more capable of helping out, for example. You can also make copies of your journal questions and these charts to keep in your journal. This way your progress is noted in one place and you can easily track how you're doing.

Here are the steps:

1. List all the rooms in your home.
2. Note the tasks needed to keep each room tidy. We'll break this down into daily, weekly, and periodically.
3. Decide who will be responsible for each task.

Here is a partial sample household chart so you can see what we're shooting for in this section. Please be creative and adjust the chart as you see fit. This is not a test you can fail. It's meant to be a creative exercise designed solely to make your life easier.

Sample Household Chart

1. List all the rooms in your home.

Entryway   Child's bedroom #1
Kitchen   Child's bedroom #2
Master bedroom   Child's bedroom #3
Master bathroom   Guest bedroom
Living room   Home office
Dining area   Front yard/porch
Den/family room   Backyard/porch
Garage

2. Note the tasks needed to keep each room tidy (broken down into daily, weekly, periodically).
3. Decide who will be responsible for each task.

continues

19

Sharing a Place Without Losing Your Space

Entryway

TASK TO BE DONE	DAILY	WEEKLY	PERIODICALLY	WHO RESPONSIBLE
Clean floor		X		
Put away coats/ gloves			X	
Dust furniture		X		

Kitchen

TASK TO BE DONE	DAILY	WEEKLY	PERIODICALLY	WHO RESPONSIBLE
Wipe stove surface	X			
Clean oven			X	
Wipe refrigerator surface		X		
Clean refrigerator (including the top!)		X		
Mop floor		X		
Wash dishes	X			
Clean sink	X			
Wipe countertops/ appliances	X			
Garbage removal	X			

Master Bedroom

TASK TO BE DONE	DAILY	WEEKLY	PERIODICALLY	WHO RESPONSIBLE
Make the bed	X			
Hang up clothes	X			
Dust furniture		X		
Return toys/ belongings to child's room (if applicable)	X			
Return dishes/glasses/ trays to kitchen (if applicable)	X			

TASK TO BE DONE	DAILY	WEEKLY	PERIODICALLY	WHO RESPONSIBLE
Vacuum		X		
Wash windows			X	

Master Bathroom

TASK TO BE DONE	DAILY	WEEKLY	PERIODICALLY	WHO RESPONSIBLE
Wipe down counters	X			
Clean toilet		X		
Clean shower/tub		X		
Mop floor		X		
Clean vanity/mirror		X		
Wash towels		X		
Empty garbage	X			
Empty hamper/ do laundry		X		

Whenever I teach my class, there is always some resistance to assigning cleaning chores, especially if children are involved. Here are some tips to help you if this is an issue in your home:

◆ Assign chores to children that are age appropriate. A five-year-old boy, for instance, might set the table rather than struggle with the family garbage at night, which his strapping teenage brother could handle without thought.

◆ If a chore is assigned and not completed, there should be consequences. Children long to be treated as adults and need to understand that chores are part of their responsibility to the family. If assignments are ignored, there will be a consequence (based on the family situation and the child, this might be no dessert after dinner, an early curfew, and so on). By the same token, rewards should be introduced into the system. I wouldn't encourage giving a child money, food, or a privilege reward every night if he washed the dishes. I would, however, assign periodic treats. Fostering a solid work ethic is a lifetime gift to your child. It can begin with washing the dinner dishes every night.

♦ Adults should communicate with each other about the division of labor in a home. I adore doing laundry, for example, and would have no trouble taking on that chore in a household with several adults. By the same token, I find no joy in washing floors or cleaning the oven. If possible, look into hiring a housekeeper to perform certain tasks.

On this last point, women often feel that cleaning is somehow their birthright and they are "less than" if they engage help. If you feel this way, I urge you to rethink your position, especially if you are mothering several children. We all have a finite amount of energy. If hiring someone even once a month to do the heavy cleaning helps restore your physical strength, you will be free to channel that energy into some nurturing, fun activities with your children.

It's also appropriate to take some special time for yourself. After all, you're keeping a journal now and I trust your daily writing time is sacred to you. What we have to give to others comes from an inner well that must be replenished. If we don't nurture and restore our own souls, the quality of our time with others will suffer. The key ingredient in your quest is balance. This is easy to write about, but I realize it can be difficult to master. Remember that mastering a difficult skill brings more joy than the easy ones.

FINAL NOTE

Getting married, moving to a new location, or any of a host of other reasons for merging households won't carry with them a magic spell that will make everyone in the new home instantly compatible. We need to craft a blueprint for the new arrangement. A balanced, well-thought-out plan will eliminate a lot of the stress inherent in such a big change.

We have a choice in our lives. We can expend our energy fighting and struggling with those we have declared we love, or we can use our energy to make a meaningful contribution to life. With the latter as our goal, the smooth running of a merged household becomes a major contributor to our goal, rather than one of the major obstacles to its achievement.

2

THE STORY OF YOUR "STUFF"

"And the day came
When the risk to remain tight in bud
Became more painful
Than the risk to bloom."

—*Anaïs Nin, American writer*

Most people collect possessions over the course of a lifetime without consciously realizing that their stuff reveals the story of their lives. The unconscious belief at work here is that holding on to relics of the past will somehow keep the past alive. It's important to review our lives before we merge them with someone else's. What are you ready to release? What treasures will you take to share? It's best if this is a conscious plan rather than a day of hurling all the worldly possessions of at least two human beings into one shared space!

Although we hold our own "stuff" sacred, we are usually ready to hurl another person's things into the trash bin with ease. How can we develop an understanding of another human being's attachments? How can we, if necessary, unearth the emotional issues held within these physical objects? Do you remember meeting Lucy in Chapter 1? She's the lady who lost her home and all of her possessions in a fire when she was five years old. Imagine someone like Lucy trying to merge a boatload of possessions with a partner who is a minimalist! The conflict isn't really over how they handle their "stuff." It is rather the effect of unresolved emotional issues.

Like Lucy, we must become detectives searching through our lives for the "secret motivators." Once uncovered, we need to understand how they have driven us. It is in this way that we can enjoy our "stuff" and not be possessed by it. It is in this way that we can understand the conflicts of our loved ones. Remember, too, that not everyone has a story as dramatic as Lucy. The seed of our need to hold on to every item as if it were a treasure may never be uncovered exactly. We need only awaken to the effect of that impulse in our lives.

YOUR STUFF, YOUR SELF

The aim in this chapter is to learn "the story of your stuff." We're going to take an inventory of your possessions and decide whether things need to stay with you or migrate to a charity, a relative, a friend, or even (gulp!) the trash bin. We'll also learn how to understand and deal effectively with personality types like the packrat, sentimental saver, procrastinator, perfectionist, and control freak. You will find help in these sections for the person with one of these issues, as well as guidance for the partner who shares the space.

Right about now you might be thinking that you don't have time to take an inventory of your belongings. You might not see the value of uncovering "the story of your stuff." Here are some practical uses for such an inventory beyond the emotional/psychological benefits:

◆ Taking inventory helps you better understand exactly what you own, before you merge your stuff with someone else's stuff.

◆ An inventory of household items is invaluable if you have homeowner's insurance. In the event you suffer a loss, filing a claim will be much easier. You might even want to photograph your jewelry and antiques and keep those photos in your safe-deposit box.

◆ The next time you have to plan a move (I'll be covering that in the next chapter), you will have more control over the process. It really doesn't have to be the most traumatic experience of your life. Moving can, in fact, provide you with an opportunity for a natural cleansing of the past (as represented by the items you choose not to take with you) and a fresh start on every level, not just the obvious physical.

Young families, for instance, move from apartments to homes and this signifies the expanding lifestyle they are creating. Conversely, retirement-age couples sell their large homes and move to condos where the upkeep is minimal and a welcome relief.

◆ You are bound to find a long lost treasure as you take inventory. My clients are forever exclaiming: "Where did you find *that?* I have been looking for it for months!" Your treasure may bring emotional comfort or a chance to make some fast cash on eBay. I'll let you decide.

TAKING INVENTORY

Let's begin by making a list of every room in your home. If you have multiple homes, let's tackle one at a time. It will be less confusing that way. If you live in a tiny studio apartment, list the areas as if they were rooms. After you have your list, let's go to each room in turn and note what is kept there. It will be helpful to have a list that breaks things down into categories. Here's a sample for you to help get your process started. Please feel free to be creative. My job is to jump-start your creative juices, not to lock you into my personal image of how this exercise should look.

Sample Room List

Kitchen	Guest Bath
Dining Area	Master Bedroom
Living Room	Master Bath
Home Office	Patio

Sample Room Inventory

Kitchen

FURNITURE, APPLIANCES	RUGS, LIGHTING FIXTURES	BOOKCASES, POSSESSIONS
Refrigerator	Ceiling fan w/light	Dishes
Stove		Glassware
Dishwasher		Pots and pans
Small appliances		Cooking tools
(toaster, coffeemaker,		Gardening tools
blender, etc.)		Vases
		Serving pieces
		Silverware

Dining Area

FURNITURE, APPLIANCES	RUGS, LIGHTING FIXTURES	BOOKCASES, POSSESSIONS
Hutch	Crystal chandelier	Good china set
Dining table with four chairs		
Two antique chairs		

Living Room

FURNITURE, APPLIANCES	RUGS, LIGHTING FIXTURES	BOOKCASES, POSSESSIONS
TV	Oriental rug	One bookcase
Wicker desk w/chair	Floor lamp	Family photos
Side table		Framed posters
Two end tables		Plants
Coffee table		
Storage trunk		
Grandfather clock		

Home Office

FURNITURE, APPLIANCES	RUGS, LIGHTING FIXTURES	BOOKCASES, POSSESSIONS
Secretary-style desk	Desk lamp	Framed art
Chair		Two bookcases
Computer		Office supplies
Printer		
Three two-drawer file cabinets		

Guest Bath

FURNITURE, APPLIANCES	RUGS, LIGHTING FIXTURES	BOOKCASES, POSSESSIONS
	Bath rug	Framed photos
		Back-up supplies (toilet paper, etc.)

Master Bedroom

FURNITURE, APPLIANCES	RUGS, LIGHTING FIXTURES	BOOKCASES, POSSESSIONS
Canopy-top double bed	Oriental rug	Antiques
Matching nightstand	Two lamps	Plants
Matching dresser		One bookcase
Side table		
One chair		
One rocker		

Note: The master suite has a walk-in closet. In addition to clothing, an extra shelf was installed on either side of the entry door for storage.

Master Bath

FURNITURE, APPLIANCES	RUGS, LIGHTING FIXTURES	BOOKCASES, POSSESSIONS
Vanity stool	Bath rug	Sundries

Patio

FURNITURE, APPLIANCES	RUGS, LIGHTING FIXTURES	BOOKCASES, POSSESSIONS
Table w/four chairs		Plants
		Garden statue of Buddha

I hope this inventory demonstrates for you how easy it is to create a document like this. You are free to go into as much detail as you like. For example, a detailed list of all the antiques could have been made. In addition, photographs or videotapes and appraisals could be kept with the homeowner's insurance policy in a safe-deposit box or a fireproof home storage container. You might even want to store electronic photos on a disc and keep that in a safe place.

In the master closet, it was noted that a second shelf had been installed for storage. You could easily make a list of the items stored there. You want to know what you have and where it is. The detailed and creative expression of this information is in your hands. I have kept it lean and simple here to encourage those timid souls who think they simply could not tackle this project. This inventory happens to be of my home. Are you ready to create your inventory? Your journal is the perfect place to begin. First, however, I would like to share a story with you about my mother.

A MOTHER'S LEGACY

When my mother was dying, she was very concerned about her things being treated with respect after she made her transition. She made it clear that *everything* was to travel with me for the rest of my life. In fact, my mother was so attached to her stuff that she saw no earthly reason for me to ever acquire my own. Hauling the possessions of her lifetime was to be my parental legacy.

My parents had moved the contents of the four-story Brooklyn brownstone I grew up in to a small house in the Allegheny Mountains outside Pittsburgh where my mother had been born. This move had been in itself a feat of engineering only my mother could have managed. After her death I was faced with the prospect of moving everything back to Brooklyn where I lived at the time. As a young woman barely out of college, I was overwhelmed. Little did I realize that the lessons I would learn over the next few years would form the philosophy that I would teach. I was in truth in training for my life's work.

I lived in Brooklyn. My mother's stuff lived in the country house. I paid the property taxes and the utility bills on a house I rarely saw. I had the three-acre lawn mowed and manicured in the summer. Once I spent a small fortune having a new roof put on the house. I felt good about these insane decisions because I was, after all, providing a safe home for my mother's stuff. Five years passed. One day I woke up.

I decided to begin the task of going through my mother's hidden possessions. You know, the ones we all have that no one sees: the photos, memorabilia, collections, and junk of a lifetime that gets stashed in drawers and hidden in storage units. The house was put on the market. Three months later a moving truck pulled into the driveway. The house was to pass to new owners. I had sifted through my mother's stuff every day for three months. It was time to move on.

The house was small but the garage and two storage units on the property were crammed with stuff. My mother was a true survivor of the depression. She kept her home immaculate but that didn't mean she didn't know how to hide her "treasures." Let me give you a vivid illustration. My mother loved the convenience of TV dinners. She made one for my school lunch break every day I was in grammar school. When she died there was a neat stack of several hundred washed TV dinner containers in the basement. "You know," she had assured me, "just in case we ever want to use them for company!" Why we would use TV dinner trays instead of the good china always escaped me, and my mother had no response. She just wanted to save them. Endless collections of this nature went into the trash.

The first thing I learned from that three months is something I tell all my clients who plead with me to understand that they just *cannot* go through their things. If you do not take care of your possessions in a responsible way, this task will fall to someone you love after your death. Make no mistake: This will not be viewed as the highlight of your earthly legacy. Most people's things are tossed away like so much garbage, but even so, someone will have the burden of having to sort through them.

I hope this story has inspired you. Here is perhaps the ultimate reason to take an inventory of your stuff. It isn't about wasting time on a meaningless exercise some professional organizer wants you to accomplish. It is rather about being responsible. It is an act of high self-esteem and a gift of love to those who will follow you.

THE FOREST AND THE TREES

If you are willing to create your inventory but feel thwarted by the state of your environment, take heart. Getting organized is a skill. In the vast majority of cases, people live in chaos because no one has ever taught them how to put a home or office together. How can you teach what you don't know? If you don't take the time to learn, who will teach your children? Getting organized can be the gift that keeps on giving in your home. Or you can elect to pass the gift of chaos on for generations to come.

Let me assure you getting organized is not rocket science. It will, however, take some dedication on your part. I know a guitarist in Los Angeles in her late 30s who dreams of being a rock star. She plays the guitar and has a band. They just never practice. They presume they will once the recording deal is signed. The trouble is life doesn't work this way. You learn a skill by taking lessons, being dedicated to the process involved, and demonstrating a willingness to practice. Getting organized is learning a skill in the same way that one learns how to play a musical instrument, masters a sport, or learns how to do craft projects.

I tell my students that Tiger Woods is one of the greatest natural talents the game of golf has ever seen. His father still gave him lessons. Not only does Tiger practice, he sometimes has bad days!

In other words, even the best practitioner of a skill is still a human being. You don't need to become the world's greatest organizer. We're in quest here of creating a nurturing environment that will comfort your very soul. Once you live in peace and calm, the work of your lifetime will be easier to accomplish. What better goal could we have to impel us through the learning curve ahead?

My clients frequently ask me if the project we are working on will be functional. They are afraid that I will make some area beautiful to look at but they will never again be able to find anything. Let's be clear. I have three goals for any project I work on and I hope you will adopt these for yourself. Your goal is to have completed projects that are …

- ◆ **Beautiful to look at.** You want to feel drawn to the space and the function to be performed there. For example, if your completed closet is still chaotic looking, why would you enjoy getting dressed? Isn't that your goal? You want to *enjoy* the spaces you bring peace to.

- ◆ **Functional.** Beauty without function is meaningless! If your closet is a joy to gaze at but you still have no idea where to find anything, you haven't completed the job. It's only part of the process if five bags of clothing go to a charity and you can't make heads or tails out of what you have decided to keep.

- ◆ **Easy to maintain.** Nothing in life is frozen in place. Life is all about change. We buy more clothes. We bring home newspapers, magazines, and business materials every day. The new items need a way to successfully merge into the system we have created.

THE MAGIC FORMULA

In upcoming chapters, we are going to examine in detail how to organize each room in a typical home. We'll look at the steps one must take to create the perfectly organized closet, lingerie drawer, kitchen pantry, or garage just to name a few. We're going to talk about useful products. I'll share some of the tips and tricks professional organizers use. Those pearls of wisdom relate, however, to the final part of the organizing process: that happy day when we are ready to put the puzzle pieces back together in a way that is beautiful, functional, and easy to maintain.

There is a process to be followed beforehand that will make this final step fun. The world of organizing has exploded in the past few years. You can research magazines, online sites, and go to any number of stores to find what's new in storage containers, clothes hangers, drawer liners, and the like (see the resources appendix at the back of this book). In fact, later on I'll make some suggestions in these areas for you. The goal is to find the solution that works for you while having fun and being creative. But before we begin, we need to take a look at the first two steps of my magical three-step formula and see that they very nicely happen simultaneously. Here are the three steps in the Magic Formula:

1. Eliminate

2. Categorize

3. Organize

It's important to understand that the whole of any project is overwhelming. You will want to break your project down into manageable, smaller-size tasks. Let's say you want to start developing your organizing skill in your home office. You walk in and one look makes you want to run screaming into the kitchen for a gallon of double chocolate ice cream and a big spoon. If you very calmly walk over to your desk and decide not to look at any other surface, you will feel the knots in your stomach relax. The room may indeed be overwhelming, but the desk is not, if only by comparison. Now you can't organize an entire desk at one time either so we're going to narrow our focus even further. It's one stack of papers at a time. You see how this works?

Let's continue with our home office example. What do you do with your stack? You make decisions about each item. Some things will, by the law of averages, be outdated and you can eliminate them. You've heard this called placing them in the "circular file." As you go through the stack, you will obviously want to hold on to some papers. As you decide to keep items, you will find that categories start to form. For example, a stack of papers on my desk would become a series of categories as I see that there are articles about the things that interest me: health, exercising, animals, travel, or perhaps my profession. Many people collect recipes and these would constitute another category.

You can create categories in every area of your home. In your pantry, it's helpful if all your soup cans are in one spot. In your closet, having all your blouses in one area saves time getting dressed. Under your bathroom sink, you might want to keep all of your hair care supplies in one container. Are you beginning to see how creative this can be and how much time you can save? You can truly eliminate questing for lost items from your daily ritual forever!

THREE STEPS TO ORGANIZING

Every organizing project involves the same three steps: eliminate, categorize, and organize. Because the first two steps happen simultaneously, you can flip them and declare yourself the CEO of your home: categorize, eliminate, and organize!

THE CHAINS THAT BIND

Most people who are challenged by their stuff find the world of organizing to be overwhelming. They feel instantly inadequate. Frequently, this is the result of early training at the hands of one parent who may have meant well but didn't have the appropriate tools to raise a child. My mother didn't mean to burden me with the possessions she had acquired over her lifetime. In her mind, she was saving me money and leaving me good quality items (think about her antiques, not her TV dinner trays) that I would enjoy for the rest of my life. She never stopped to consider that she was stifling my creativity and denying me the acquisition journey she had taken in her life. Parents mean well. They just happen to be human beings.

Just as you now feel inadequate in these waters, your parents may have been at a loss. Can't relate to this? You grew up in a perfectly organized home? There was a place for everything and everything was always in its place? What about your mate? What kind of upbringing did he or she have? The next time you find socks tossed around the bedroom floor like seashells on a beach, take a step back before you get angry. Instead of recriminations like: "Why can't you *ever* put dirty clothes in the hamper? Why do *I* have to pick up after you?" why not take the time to understand? If someone approaches me and tells me why something is important to him, I am far more likely to respond positively than if I am attacked. You might even decide that your newfound understanding has made you happy to pick up those socks!

I am reminded of a wonderful couple I worked with years ago. Rick and Diane were both high paid, power-wielding execs in separate industries. Diane's success came in a male-dominated industry. She was multilingual specializing in hard-to-master languages. Rick was lauded in another industry for his creativity and ingenuity. I really liked them both.

Rick made no secret, however, that he *never* lifted a finger around the house. He would make it a point *not* to put down the toilet seat or hang up his clothes. Rick joked, "I would drive you crazy, wouldn't I, Regina?" I assured him he would. I asked him why Diane put up with his behavior. It seemed to me that he treated her like a maid (although I assure you they had one of those floating about the house on a daily basis).

Rick laughed and gave me an answer I never forgot. "I want to be the king of my castle, Regina. And my wife gets compensated in other ways. For instance, I have no idea how much money she makes or what she does with it. I presume she has a bundle stashed in some bank. I pay all the bills. Every year I take her on a fabulous trip. And every year without fail a brand-new Jag appears in the driveway." I got it. It wouldn't work for me, but I had to admire the way this couple had artfully worked out the domestic details of their marriage. There is no foolproof blueprint for what works. You'll have to negotiate that for yourself. In this couple's case, Diane enjoyed taking care of her husband and found it a break from the rigors of corporate America.

THE SECOND TIME AROUND

Very often the most challenging home mergers are those of the second marriage. You not only have had more time to collect stuff, you have also had an experience of sharing a previous home. This can sometimes work against you by setting up preconceived notions of how things "should" be the second time around. Let's meet a couple I worked with recently. See if you identify with them.

Joan and Bob recently got married. Now in their 40s, they were each previously married quite young and have six children between them. Sorting delicately through their possessions to create a new home took love, patience, and guidance. For example, having raised sons, Bob had little understanding of how to deal with the seemingly exploding array of lotions and potions young girls have in their bathroom. He needed to learn how to communicate his displeasure when sticky residue was left on the countertop.

The girls, in turn, needed to find a way to organize their possessions so that they had access to what they owned and needed without taking over the entire room. As you can see, no one was being difficult in this situation. Communication was the key to finding a working solution. So often, we presume the other person understands our position and our feelings and he or she has simply chosen to be difficult. More often than not, the other party is thinking the same thing about our behavior! When love and respect form the foundation of a relationship, communication can heal most of the everyday problems and wounds.

COMING FULL CIRCLE

Right about now you may be wondering about that inventory list you worked on earlier in the chapter. How can it help you when you move? What service will it perform when you have to merge your belongings with those of another? If you have already done the latter, how can this exercise assist you as you try to make sense out of the confusion? We're ready to find out.

All my stories up to this point were meant to illustrate one point. Stuff always has a story. It has a life of its own for some people. I told you that at the beginning, but like most people your knee jerk reaction was probably, "Oh! Not my stuff! It's just there!" Here are some exercises to help you not only understand what the contents of your inventory mean but how you may want to deal with them now that you understand their origin better.

Please take some time to answer the following questions in your journal. All your answers should be based on what you listed in your inventory.

1. Do you have any possessions from a time in your life that is past? For example, are you a new parent still holding on to the relics of your college dorm life?

2. Is your house filled with the possessions of others? These can be inherited items from a deceased friend or relative or you might discover that you have agreed to hold on to things for family and friends. How many parents wish their grown children would claim the possessions they left in the home of their childhood?

3. Have you outgrown or changed styles and wish that you could off load some items that no longer reflect who you are and how you wish to express yourself? I grew up with Colonial American furniture. When my parents passed away, I inherited the furniture of my youth and believed I liked it all. Imagine my surprise when I realized that I was drawn to the furniture of the Western United States.

4. Are there any items in your inventory that are listed with a one-word description ("photos" would be a classic example) that actually stand for boxes and boxes of the item in question? Can you sort through your collection and bring some order to it? In the case of photos, you have several choices: organize them into photo albums (or hire a consultant to do this), share the extra prints with family and friends, toss the photos you don't like and know you will never display.

5. Are there any items in your home that cause other family members to be upset? How important is that item to you? Is it in reality worth the discomfort it causes a loved one? Gentlemen, let me say here that no photos of ex-loves should be on display! And ladies, let's not have any letters from previous loves casually propped on the dresser. These items are for your memorabilia box.

   I had a client whose new husband hung a remnant from his bachelor days—a wall clock with a portrait of John Wayne—in their bedroom opposite the bed. "I would wake up each morning with John Wayne staring me in the face, larger than life," the wife said. A little pre-move-in work with an inventory would have eliminated this problem. (By the way, John Wayne doesn't hang there anymore!)

6. Do you have items in your home that remind you of times past? It's wonderful to honor our lives and our loved ones but it's also crucial to remember that no object is a magic talisman that can return us to our past. I am reminded of the client who rued the day she gave away the yellow rain slickers her sons had worn the year they lived abroad. Those slickers were part of her memory of seeing her sons as children waiting for the school bus. When she shared this story with me, her sons were now men in their 30s. Mourning the loss of those slickers was a cover for the real issue: She wanted to be that young mother again, not a grandmother in her early 60s. No item can restore the past. Longing for times gone by prevents us from being fully invested in the present moment.

If you answer these questions honestly, I have no doubt you will be amazed by what you learn. Imagine for a minute that you awaken in a dark room. You have no idea where you are or how you got there. Your first desire is to escape. You try by feeling your way along the wall. Suddenly, someone opens the door and the room is flooded with light. You look around you and see you are in an empty room. There was no reason to be afraid. The light makes it easier to exit the room with ease. The light also removes any fear you might have experienced. You imagined goblins. The room is actually empty. In much the same way, these questions shed light on areas of emotional darkness in your consciousness.

Please feel free to insert your own questions in an area that feels like it is yielding answers to the clutter in your life. For example, let's consider the first question. Are you shocked to find that you are stuck in the college experience? Why not do some additional journaling about this phenomena and how it affects your life? Here are some examples of questions you might ask yourself:

- Am I happy today with my life?
- Do I believe that life was better when I was in school? Why?
- What fear is behind this belief?
- Is it time to decorate my living quarters in a more adult manner?

There are no rules. You can't make a mistake. Each journey is personal and unique. It's also prudent to realize that you may decide to embark on a particular organizing project after working in your journal. Please schedule this project in your calendar just as you would a project at work or lunch with a friend. We succeed in life in direct proportion to the respect we pay our endeavors.

When you first create your inventory list you will probably look at it and be content with everything on it. After a few organizing projects are completed, you'll find that some items will be removed from the list. You might be shocked by the sense of relief that overcomes you. I wouldn't be surprised if you lose a few pounds. As you begin to examine the emotional issues underlying the collection of stuff you now hold sacred, you may find the courage to further whittle away at the list.

When I finally moved my parents' belongings back to Brooklyn, it had taken three months to go through everything they left behind. I said after that experience that I could move without notice because "if you see it, you know I want it." That experience taught me how to live a streamlined life, why it was invaluable and led me to a place where I could extol its virtues to others. Please don't feel guilty for an instant, by the way, if you discover that you have willingly been saddled up to now with items you really don't want. Life isn't about making perfect decisions. Life is about growth. I believe there are no accidents. You will wake up to a new reality when you are ready. And it will touch the lives of everyone close to you. In this way we are truly each other's teachers and students.

PERSONALITY TYPES WE KNOW AND LOVE

Some people might realize that they have deeper issues to deal with. I am going to touch briefly here on some major personality types. These good people have more of a challenge getting organized than most. Entire books have been written about each of these issues, so please realize that our endeavor here is to jump start the healing process. It has taken time to get stuck in a negative pattern. It will take time to solve the problem and create a more positive reality. In the best of all possible worlds, my words would be all you need. More likely, you might need to speak to someone like a religious cleric or a therapist. You could join a support group. You might need the assistance of a medical doctor. I encourage you to take advantage of whatever tools you need. In my parents' day, no one acknowledged they needed help. It was cause for shame. Can you imagine? How fortunate we are that help is available to everyone who wants to change for the better.

These personality types might also reflect the partner you have chosen to share your life with. It is helpful to understand these issues. People aren't procrastinators or packrats for the fun of it. They will not heal through our anger or judgment. They will, however, be impacted by the depth of our love, the greatest healing force in the universe. If you find yourself living with a packrat or procrastinator, the two most interesting questions for you to answer are: Why were you attracted to someone with this issue, and what do you get out of the power struggle that inevitably ensues? We all get something out of the conflicts we create. It is helpful to understand these issues. People aren't procrastinators or packrats for the fun of it. They will not heal through our anger or judgment. While your partner is busy unraveling the origins of a difficult problem, you can be working on yourself. In this way you can inspire each other.

Are you ready? Let's begin our review.

THE PACKRAT

If I had a dollar for every person who has ever confessed to me that he or she is a packrat, I could retire to the French Riviera. If your home is a hotbed of chaos, it might not have anything to do with your being a packrat. It is more likely that you have no idea how to get organized.

Here's a brief quiz to help you identify your problem. Let's see if you are truly a packrat, shall we? Please answer yes or no:

- ◆ Do you find yourself unable to toss old newspapers and magazines?
- ◆ Are newspapers and magazines in fact piling up in every available space in your home?
- ◆ Do you look around you and see an inordinate amount of shopping bags filled with newspapers, magazines, and books?

◆ Even though you do not have the time to read this material, are you unable to stop yourself from bringing more into the home?

◆ Do these purchases jeopardize your finances in any way? Do you spend money on reading matter that should go to the food budget or the rent?

◆ Are there rooms you are literally not able to enter because they are filled with bags and boxes of stuff?

◆ Is there a pathway through any part of your home just wide enough for you to place one foot in front of the other?

The average person who incorrectly labels himself a packrat will have a majority of "no" responses. He or she will in fact wonder why I asked such extreme questions. The true packrat will however recognize himself or herself in these questions. The response will more likely be, "How did you know?"

Being a packrat is one of the many manifestations of Obsessive Compulsive Disorder known commonly as OCD. It is frequently accompanied by an extreme fear of germs. If this is your issue, you can best be helped by investing some time in therapy with someone who specializes in OCD. Your therapist can also inform you about drugs specifically designed for treating this disorder.

It's important to understand that you will require outside professional help to overcome your particular challenge with stuff. No amount of rationalizing, explaining, or intellectual hypotheses will enable you to recover. They can, however, be effective once therapy has commenced. Understand, too, that this is not your fault. People frequently become angry with the packrat as if he or she enjoys the inability to stop stockpiling stuff in the home. Does the diabetic enjoy his challenge with sugar? Is the cancer patient delighted he can undergo chemotherapy? The packrat is no less powerless and miserable. Paradoxically, of course, although the piles are disturbing, they also offer comfort. As human beings we can buffer our life experience with all manner of things. Physical stuff and extra body weight are two of the classic choices.

Frank is a respected member of his community. His outward appearance is always fastidious. Frank and his wife June, however, have not entertained guests in more than 20 years. No one is allowed to enter their home, not even their three grown sons. You see, only a narrow pathway leads you through the house. Every available surface is covered with the debris of ancient newspapers, magazines, and innumerable items from Frank's various hobbies. "Stuff" has shut out the world.

CROSSING THE LINE

If your personal collections are inching out your family and friends from your environment, you are probably a packrat. It isn't an insurmountable problem, but it does require professional help to overcome.

If you're living with a packrat like Frank, I have some journal questions for you. Spouses frequently act as if this trait is a complete surprise to them. More likely is the fact that you assumed the person would change after you got married or moved in together. This fantasy is fed to us in popular movies on a regular basis. A man and a woman with enormous problems meet and within minutes decide they are soul mates. Once they are together, all those problems they were carrying around like bags of rocks magically vanish. It really is a disservice to the audience.

Here are some journal questions for the packrat's partner.

1. When did you first notice these symptoms in your partner?
2. How did you view what you saw? For example, did you think there were piles everywhere because of a busy schedule at work?

3. Did you think things would change when you moved in together? How? Did you imagine your partner would alter his/her behavior because of your presence? Or did you plan to become the one who would pick up the environment?

4. How does the constant mess make you feel?

5. Are the feelings you noted familiar to you? For example, if you said you feel frustrated and angry all the time, is that how felt in your home of origin as a child? Sometimes we don't consciously like a feeling but it becomes so familiar that we find a clever (albeit unconscious) way to recreate it in our new surroundings.

Piles of books, newspapers, and magazines can be debilitating visually, emotionally, and mentally. If the packrat seeks help, it is comforting to know that rather than being judged, their partner is trying to change the habit patterns that drew him or her into this dynamic in the first place. One of my teachers once said something I never forgot: There are no victims, only volunteers.

Before we leave this section, I want to share an image with you. The illustration that follows is a sketch of an office I cleaned out for a packrat. She hadn't used the office in years. It is one of many spaces around Los Angeles that are rented to house newspapers, magazines, books, and other assorted items. Releasing this space was the first step this person was willing to take. For those of you who incorrectly label yourselves packrats because of an occasional pile or two around the house during the school year, take heart. If you identify with this illustration, though, remember that help is available to you. Your willingness to change your life is the first indispensable key to a new way of life.

Let's move on now and take a look at some other personality types that can cause havoc in the home landscape.

Here's a view of a typical packrat's office.

THE SENTIMENTAL SAVER

One day I was working with a wife while her husband was out of town on a business trip. Rachel felt it would be a lovely surprise if Ron returned home to a streamlined master bedroom closet. The closet was a walk-in but not in any way adequate for two adults. I noticed that a guest closet in the downstairs had some space. They liked to entertain and felt this area should be set aside for the needs of their guests. I pointed out that they lived in the house on a daily basis and their needs had to come first. Their master closet was about to burst. No other closet in the house offered any assistance. Rachel finally agreed.

As we began the process of deciding which items might make the big migration downstairs an interesting fact became apparent. Ron was a very sentimental man. He had obviously led a successful life filled with wonderful memories. Unfortunately, personalized T-shirts, jackets, and baseball caps accompanied those memories from every project. The movie and television industries are famous for rewarding cast and crewmembers with all manner of souvenirs emblazoned with the trademark of the production.

By the way, we all tend to do a version of Ron's collecting. Do you have every airline receipt, movie ticket stub, and restaurant menu from your last trip? Or perhaps you inherited all of your parents' possessions. I had a client whose basement looked like a furniture warehouse. No one in the family wanted their parents' furniture. At the same time no one wanted to give any of it away. So it was transported from Florida to New York in order to live in my client's basement!

While I am not an unsentimental person, I realize that I cannot keep every potential keepsake that crosses my path. If you aren't ever realistically going to look at or do anything with your treasures, it might be time to streamline. Don't think of this as an act of losing something you cherish. Take the best souvenir from a trip or a late loved one and enjoy it. Share the wealth. Do you know of a charity or a friend who needs some of the extra clothing and furniture in your home? Could you sell some of your treasures online at a site like eBay and make some extra money? Don't need money? Donate what you make to your favorite charity.

If you are the collector in the family, consider these ideas and start slowly. If you feel guilty for even considering a new future for some of your items, it might be worth your while to do some journaling about this issue. Here are some journal questions to get you started. You may discover a hidden fear, a consciousness of loss, or an internalized parental instruction. You are the architect of your life experience. I know you will make a good choice! No one has to be permanently saddled with an unconsciously driven negative habit. Remember: "There are no victims, only volunteers."

Here are some journal questions for the sentimental reader.

1. What kinds of items are you drawn to keeping? Are you a furniture collector? Do you hold on to every travel souvenir? Are there one too many antiques in your home? Please be specific about what attracts you and why.

2. When did you begin collecting your items? Were your parents sentimental? Do you presume you inherited this trait? Or as the child of completely unsentimental parents, are you in rebellion to the way you were raised? It's helpful to uncover the origin of your need to save. Remember how my mother told me to keep all of her things? I moved every item from Pennsylvania where she and my father had retired back to New York. In a few months I hauled it all out to California. Can you imagine how much money I spent on movers?

3. If your collections spill out all over the house, do you understand why your partner is annoyed? Can you take a step back and see how unfair this behavior is? Are you willing to alter the physical environment to make everyone who lives with you more comfortable? You have many choices: Eliminate some items, keep the remaining ones in controlled areas of the home, and/or find offsite storage for all your treasures.

If you are the unsentimental partner of a natural saver, your questions will be along these lines.

1. Did you realize the natural propensity to save in your partner from the beginning? When did you realize what was happening?

2. How do these collections affect you and the environment? Are you out of closet space because the shelves have become storehouses for souvenirs? Is the coffee table, nightstand, or kitchen counter a constant eyesore? What specific changes could you suggest to your partner that

> would honor your needs in the environment while simultaneously honoring their natural propensity?
>
> 3. Are you willing to work out a compromise or has this become a power struggle? Are you the kind of person who needs to win? If this issue is cleared up, will another take its place because of an underlying power struggle in the relationship?

So often I find that surface issues are merely the tools we use to work out deeper issues. In general, the "space problems" I encounter as an organizer have one of two origin points: Either the problem arises because the client is ignorant of the proper way to get organized or the client has unconsciously decided to use his space to work out an emotional issue. If you can get to the bottom of your challenge with stuff and space, you can restore peace and contentment to your very soul.

THE PERFECTIONIST AND THE PROCRASTINATOR

You might be surprised to find these two personality archetypes in one section. They seem like polar opposites, don't they? I refer to these two personalities as twins born of the marriage of Fear of Success and Fear of Failure. They are, in truth, opposite sides of the same coin. Let's take a look at each.

My sympathy for the perfectionist is due to the fact that I am myself a recovered perfectionist. The clear message in my home, as a child, was to do things perfectly or to not bother at all. A story I tell in my classes illustrates my parents' philosophy perfectly. I was in the first or second grade when this incident happened. My mother always grilled me about other children's grades. She did my homework with me every night until I was letter perfect. I lived in a world of competition and comparisons. It was exhausting. This day I had a midterm report card to show my mother. All the way home I had a spring in my step. I had managed to achieve the highest grade in the class. There would be celebrating in my home tonight. I would be off the hook. Even now I can remember entering the family room and seeing my mother. She was sitting in a big leather chair engrossed in *The New York Times*. I triumphantly handed my report card to my mother when she asked for it.

As my mother began the usual litany of "What did so and so get?" I stopped her. I proudly announced that I had the highest grade in the class. No one had done better than the 96 displayed on my card. My mother's next words stunned me. Unfortunately, I was too young to have the verbal and emotional skills to respond. She said simply, "Only 100 is good enough." With that she handed me the report card and vanished behind *The New York Times*. I was stunned. How many times could I achieve 100? The vise of perfection tightened around my soul.

As an adult with more than 12 years of therapy under my belt, I now understand that my parents' true goals were to foster a desire for excellence in my life. What they inadvertently did was to make me shy away from any experience I was not certain I could master from the outset. The perfectionist is riddled with fear. What if you attempt something and you don't succeed? The shame knows no bounds. You feel it is better to do what you can perfectly and ignore the rest. Unfortunately, this leaves a lot of unexplored territory in life. If this is your challenge, let me share how, in addition to therapy, I conquered the hold perfection had in my life.

I am a graceful woman. I love to exercise. I am not, however, by any stretch of the imagination an athletic woman. Put me in a pool, on a tennis court or on skis and voilà—an uncoordinated geek appears! I decided to study the martial arts. Here was a world I was guaranteed I could not master. I would never be the best student in the class. Why did I do it? Every week for two years my only goal was to perform better than I had the previous week. I learned the difference between doing something "perfectly" and doing it to the best of your ability. The former is impossible. No human is perfect, and neither are the fruits of his labors. Everyone, however, can grow and develop a skill. The guys in my class frequently asked why I bothered to return each week. I couldn't begin to explain how what they perceived to be a poor performance was in fact a victory for my soul. The little girl whose report card was not adequate for her parents, had learned to please herself.

Here are some journal questions to ponder if you feel that the quest for perfection is part of your life.

1. Have you always been a perfectionist?

2. Did your parents encourage this behavior or did you develop it as a result of some life experience? Imagine, for example, an adult who isn't particularly secure within herself who one day discovers she has a natural talent for cooking and cleaning. Instead of this being a gift to the family, it can be the means this person uses to control the environment. See if you can discover the origin of your quest for perfection.

3. What do you think you get out of your quest for perfection? Is it a way to make you feel superior? Is it a way to control others? Does it enable you to sit in judgment of others?

4. Would you like to change? Draw a line down a fresh page in your journal and create two columns. On the left side, make a list of the ways your need to be perfect manifests itself. In the adjacent column, list all the ways you could change your behavior.

As you can probably imagine, I used to be a devoted housekeeper. In my 20s and 30s I think I did the equivalent of spring-cleaning each weekend. Guess where I learned this behavior? One day I realized that this was crazy. I enjoy a clean home but I was turning down social engagements to clean. Want to know what I did? I got a Golden Retriever! I had grown up with a dog and longed to have one again. Once you have pets, you can kiss a perfect environment good-bye. I would rather have the love of my dog and an imperfect environment than the pristine setting I used to have without my best friend. It's only one of many ways to learn how to relax. What will you do?

Let's move on now to the perfectionist's twin, the procrastinator. His or her life is no bed of roses. The fear of failure unconsciously turns every activity into a drama. The procrastinator is late for appointments. Work or school assignments are turned in at the last minute. Friends are left waiting on street corners and in restaurants. The procrastinator buys calendars and self-help books but never has time to use them. He or she is the unconscious star of the show (remember Marilyn from Chapter 1?). When we live a life fueled by a rush of adrenaline, we can become addicted to the high it produces. Add to this the underlying fears involved and you can see why this isn't an easy fix.

Here are some journal questions designed to help the procrastinator uncover not only the roots of the issue but the underlying fears.

1. Have you always been prone to delaying tasks? If your answer if yes, how did your parents react to this behavior? Were they in fact procrastinators who taught you how to behave this way? Or in retrospect was this a way for you to attract attention from one or more siblings?

2. If this is a newly acquired behavior, when did it start? Was it, for example, after a forced move to a new locale to suit the professional needs of your partner? Did it begin after a death in the family when you were feeling overwhelmed in general? Please try and identify your "start date" and be as specific and descriptive as you feel comfortable.

3. How does your behavior make you feel? What effect does it have on your family, co-workers, and friends?

4. What do you think you are able to avoid with all of this extra energy you expend? Are you, for example, afraid of

more responsibility at work or of disappointing a superior who believes in you?

5. Can you pinpoint a goal that habitually gets put on the back burner because of your delaying tactics? How important is that goal to you?

6. What five steps could you take to change your ways? Be specific, and understand that you need not tackle all of them at one time! Some suggestions include reading more about time management, purchasing an organizing system that works (electronic gadget, paper calendar/organizer, etc.), asking someone to be your "responsibility buddy" and hold you accountable until you can take care of yourself, joining a 12-step program for procrastinators, working with a therapist or professional organizer, and identifying true/neglected goals and taking one step in the direction of fulfilling that dream.

If you are the partner of a procrastinator, the basic questions are the same.

1. When did you first notice this trait in your partner?

2. If it happened early in the relationship, did you presume you could change him or her?

3. What do you think you get out of having to deal with this problem?

4. Did you grow up in a household with similar issues? Is it possible you created this situation because on some level it makes you feel comfortable, superior, or needed?

5. How have you tried to deal with this situation in the past? Please be specific and make a list. How effective were these efforts?

6. Name two new things you could do to help the situation. For example, you might experiment with some private

and/or couples counseling. The former allows you to uncover what attracted you to a situation that irritates you and the latter will provide some tools in healing the home dynamic. Or ask your partner if there are ways you could help that would be appreciated.

LESSONS FROM THE PAST

As a young woman, I specialized in dating the "bad boy." Every woman reading this book will recognize the man I am referring to. He's the dashing, funny, extremely sexy, highly unavailable man who appears at every social gathering. His unavailability is emotional—that is, he is so afraid of commitment and attached to himself that he is present in body only. His ego is so self-serving that there is no room for anyone else. My therapist once summed up a rocky relationship I was in this way: "The thing you and John have in common is that you are both in love with him!" Ouch!

When friends listened to the saga of my dating life, whether it was John, Joe, Harry, or Frank, they always sided with me. "Regina, you are so sweet. What's wrong with these guys?" As you might guess, the problem actually lay within me. I was afraid of a relationship that might end in marriage. What if I duplicated my parents' marriage? What if grown up responsibilities took me away from my creative pursuits? Instead of fixing what was broken inside myself, I turned my energy into fixing every broken "bad boy" who crossed my path.

In much the same way, some of you may have attached yourself to the packrat, the procrastinator, the perfectionist—the list is endless—in an effort to escape dealing with your own issues. It's a great way to avoid what is broken within our own soul. It brings us attention we may not know how to get otherwise. We are the hero or heroine of a self-created drama. In truth, we cannot heal anyone else. We can only take care of and heal ourselves. I promise you that in time the peace that fills your soul will be as addictive as the drama that now envelops you.

THE CONTROL FREAK

One day a client confided in me about her new husband. I was planning to write this book and was especially interested in second-time-around couples and the challenges unique to their situations. Colette shared an anecdote with me that made me smile. It illustrates the work of a well-meaning albeit unconscious control freak. We tend to think of control freaks as we see them depicted in movies and on TV. In a fantasy situation they need to behave in extreme ways. In life, the control they try to wield is usually doled out in more subtle ways. Let me share the story Colette told me that day.

Sam is a very thoughtful husband. He's the kind of man we all dream about marrying: He lives to anticipate his family's needs. One thing he did, however, caused some annoyance and Colette was trying to figure out how to address the issue with him. It seemed that Sam did all the grocery shopping for the new family. The cupboards were never bare. Sam was so attentive to detail, in fact, that items would be restocked just as they were about to run out. No one ever needed a shopping list in this house! In fact, that was the crux of the matter!

Everyone wanted to be asked what he or she needed or wanted from the store. Frequently items that had not been enjoyed would reappear. By assuming that replacing the existing stock was all that was required, Sam was dropping the ball. In fact, the cupboard at their new house was stocked when his bride's moving truck drove up to the house. Sam had silently made a study of what Colette and her children ate by checking out the cabinets in their old home!

My advice to Colette was to tread lightly in this territory. Sam was in my estimation an unwitting control freak. His motives were good. He was attempting to make everyone in the new home happy. Sam's heart was in the right place. But he needed to be told that everyone wanted a say in what food was brought into the home. Family members wanted to be able to tell him what they wanted and what they didn't. By deciding that he knew best, Sam was unwittingly short-circuiting the family dynamic. Colette and her children felt powerless and controlled rather than loved. It would not be long before he would be making decisions on his own in other areas of family life. The moral of this story: If you don't speak up, the other person can only presume you enjoy not participating in the decision-making process.

Here are some questions for you to answer in your journal if you feel you might be a control freak.

1. Did you relate to Sam in this story? What things do you do that remind you of his behavior? Please be specific. What are your motives?

2. Taking a step back, can you place yourself in the shoes of your family members? How, in other words, would you feel if someone behaved in this way toward you?

3. Do you ask your family what they want in these situations or have you presumed?

4. Would you be able to share control of each situation with family members? Sam, for example, could have done the shopping once a week and asked his new family at the dinner table what was on their food wish list.

5. Were decisions made for you in your family of origin? How did you feel about that? Did you learn that part of being an adult was making decisions for others?

6. What do you hope to gain by doing things for others without consulting with them?

7. If you abandoned this behavior, what is it you would lose?

As you know by now, it takes two to tango. Here are your journal questions if you are living with a control freak.

1. Did you grow up in a household that encouraged you to make your own decisions or was your day-to-day life pretty much mapped out for you?

2. Is it possible that being controlled reminds you of your family of origin? We frequently re-create situations (even uncomfortable and undesirable ones) because the emotional responses they elicit are comforting to us. What's that old saying? "The devil you know is better than the devil you haven't met."

3. In your previous relationships, was control an issue? Is it manifesting now in a familiar pattern?

4. When did you first sense that your partner had a tendency to control?

5. What was your initial reaction? Have you addressed it with him or her? Do you get a satisfactory response? How would you like to resolve this issue?

When I think about my own family of origin, one of my sweetest memories is how my parents shared responsibility for the home. My father did the laundry and the grocery shopping. He felt he did those tasks better than my mother. For her part, my mother cleaned a four-story brownstone each week. Her plate was full. My father knew my mother wasn't home eating bonbons and watching TV while he shopped and did laundry!

I clearly remember daily discussions of what was to be made for dinner and what groceries were needed. These communications were a form of intimacy, part of a daily dance my parents performed. I share this because you can learn to make communicating about anything part of the intimacy you experience in your relationship. We tend to think that intimacy is sexual in nature. We fail to realize that sex is only a part of what is truly an intricate mosaic called intimacy. If you are trying to control your family life, you are missing opportunities to bond. I hope you will experiment with altering family roles and responsibilities in your home. My father was probably the only man in our Brooklyn neighborhood who routinely shopped and did laundry. Trust me—no one ever questioned his masculinity!

FINAL NOTE

Planning is perhaps the key ingredient when we are about to embark on the adventure of sharing an environment with another human being. Your inventory is at once a practical and an emotional tool. Once you have it, you will be able to move to a new location and merge your possessions with another's with greater ease. An inventory enables us to see what we have. It also enables us to understand why we have it. Human beings will always have conflict. Without conflict no movie, play, or story is of any interest! Our emotional issues need not be hidden behind the veil of our possessions.

This chapter calls for some soul searching and will take some time to work through. The results, however, will serve you long after you have read the last page of this book. The end result of this work is a home with an environment that not only nurtures the occupants but all those who come to visit.

3

MOVING DOESN'T HAVE TO BE A DIRTY WORD!

"Failing to plan is planning to fail."
—Ben Franklin

Long before the moving truck delivers all of your life treasures to your new home, you and your partner need to do some organizing. I can't tell you how many couples get into trouble because they assume that the other person feels the same way they do about their possessions. I might love the dishes I inherited from my mother. There is no guarantee anyone else will!

How do you deal with things you'd rather not live with? What happens when there are perfectly respectable yet multiple sets of everyday dishes, toasters, and blenders? What are the merits and pitfalls of outside storage? Whew! Let's start at the beginning and see if we can't use our inventory list from the previous chapter to help craft a move that will run smoothly and not drain our physical, emotional, and financial resources.

I'll cover the basics in this chapter, but if you'd like more tips and strategies on moving, you might want to check out *The Complete Idiot's Guide to Smart Moving* by Dan Ramsey (Alpha Books, 1998).

SELECTING A MOVER

One day I was talking to a neighbor who was busy getting ready for her move. "Did you select a mover yet?" I asked. She said she had not and wanted to know if I had anyone I would recommend. I said there was only one mover in Los Angeles whose name I gave out to people. This lady wanted to know what his fees were. I said he was about $10 more an hour than other movers and worth every penny. She told me she intended to hire the cheapest mover she could find. I wished her well.

A few weeks later, as luck would have it, I was exiting our building as my neighbor's movers were loading the truck. As I walked out of the front door, one of the movers picked up a box from a dolly and quite literally hurled it onto the truck. The shattering of glass could clearly be heard. I knew my neighbor had made a common mistake. She believed that anyone with a truck could safely move belongings. Nothing could be farther from the truth!

TIME IS MONEY

You will be paying your movers by the hour. The more information you can supply up front, the less time you will have to stop throughout the moving day and answer questions. Saving time means saving money.

When you are looking for a mover, you will want to call several companies to get bids. It's a good idea to compare bids so that you are sure the mover you decide on is in the ballpark when it comes to charges. Large moving companies will also give you free literature that can prove invaluable during your planning phase.

Here are some things to consider during your interview:

◆ How long have they been in business? Do they have references you could contact? If you found their number in the Yellow Pages, check with the Better Business Bureau to be sure they haven't received any letters of complaint about this company.

◆ Is the representative who comes to your home the owner of the company or an employee?

◆ You'll want to give this person as many details as you can. The more he understands your situation, the more equitable the estimate will be. Remember, however, that the men who appear on moving day have probably not read the estimate. You should expect to explain everything to them as well. Don't assume they know. I frequently hear clients exclaim to one of the worker bees on moving day: "But I already went through all this!"

◆ Who will be in charge of your move? The day of the move the moving company will designate one of the men as the captain of the team who will be in charge of the proceedings. If you are making a long move across state lines, the driver of the truck is usually the owner of his rig. He will be in charge of your belongings on the road. At the new location, he will supervise the men or women who appear to assist in unloading the truck.

◆ Ask your representative if they "job in" help when needed or if they have an adequate staff. In the best of all possible worlds, you want the latter scenario to be the case. You know you'll be working with guys who do this day in and day out for a living rather than from time to time to make some extra money.

◆ Will your household items be loaded onto a truck and then unloaded at the new location? Or will they be taken to a warehouse for transfer to a different rig? Remember that every time your things are moved, the chance of breakage or damage increases. You want them placed on one truck. When my best friend moved to another state, she forgot to ask about this. She presumed that a small load placed on a small truck would go directly to the new destination.

Surprise! A completely different driver and truck showed up at the new house. Her entire inventory had been loaded onto a new truck for transfer across state lines.

◆ Your mover will offer you insurance. Check your existing homeowners policy first. You might already be covered for the move. If you do purchase special insurance, remember that you are best covered if the movers do your packing. If something breaks in a Packed by Owner box, the coverage is less. The company might even challenge it.

◆ Movers are professionals. They pack things for a living. I encourage my clients to let them handle this task, if possible. It is physically draining and I think you want to reserve your strength for the new home. If you are one of those good people who simply must participate in the process, let the movers pack the breakables and you can pack the unbreakable items (books, bedding, towels, etc.).

◆ Invest in some boxes at a box store or directly from your moving company. If you do your own packing, don't make the boxes too heavy. Too many books, for instance, in one huge box might give your mover a hernia. A cranky mover is not a productive mover. When you are getting your estimate, be sure and state which items you intend to pack. The representative writing the order will take that into account, as it will reduce the allotted time the movers need to have at your home of origin.

◆ Remember that everything that is to be moved and packed has to be revealed to the movers during the initial session. Your estimate will be affected if you constantly add and subtract items and locations.

Speaking of locations, if you have furniture and boxes going to separate addresses (for example, you want some items given to a friend and others taken to storage) you need to be specific with your mover. Again, changes you make will affect your estimate and the final bill.

PROFESSIONAL ORGANIZERS TO THE RESCUE

Don't let your movers unpack your boxes in the new location! They will quite literally unpack you. While your home will be free of boxes and wrapping paper, you will have an unorganized sea of possessions surrounding you. If the thought of unpacking your own boxes is overwhelming, enlist the help of a professional organizer; these folks specialize in all phases of moving.

YOU GET WHAT YOU PAY FOR

A few years ago one of my favorite clients was moving to a new house. Frederick has a propensity for large homes and lots of exquisite possessions. This was a move for my favorite mover! What makes him the only mover I recommend to people? First of all the business is a family-run operation. The current owner's father started it and worked side by side with his son in the field. Now his son is an adult with three grown sons of his own. The middle son works in the office while the oldest and the youngest work as movers. There are two additional gentlemen who work in the field packing and hauling boxes and furniture. They are all clean-cut guys. Their attention to detail, the pride they have in their work, and the care they extend to each client makes me proud to refer them. They are so close to perfect, in fact, I call them my choirboys! (They are Stratton & Son Moving and Storage; see the appendix for more information about the areas they service.)

I remember once, years before I found my ideal company, I was working with another mover. Every job was a crapshoot. I never had any idea who would show up at the job site. The straw that broke the camel's back was the day they sent a new supervisor. He was capable. He also looked like a refugee from the band Kiss. Long dark hair flowed nearly to his waist. His muscle T-shirt and short shorts let everyone know he worked out. I was grateful my client was on a movie location and never saw him. I like to maintain a certain professional decorum.

My current movers take care of you as if you were a member of their family. You are treated with respect and so are your possessions. No one in this group would ever hurl a box onto a truck or take anything that didn't belong to him. I treasure honesty and a true work ethic. When we moved my client to his new home, Frederick remembered a tiny medal that had been attached to his office bulletin board. It was a treasure from his childhood. It had belonged to his late father who passed away when my client was only four. It was irreplaceable. I assured him that the medal would turn up. He was certain the movers had tossed it, if only in error. I held my breath as we unpacked his new office. The medal was nowhere to be found. My client was crestfallen and I was in shock. How could my guys have missed that medal?

Can you guess what happened? My guys had taken the medal off the bulletin board and wrapped it with some other tiny items. They were tucked into a decorative box that had not been opened. When I found it, I said nothing to my client. I walked up to the master suite and attached it to his pillow with a note. Working with the best, even if it costs a few extra dollars, is worth it. Frederick agreed!

In contrast, I want to share the story of Philip. A dashing Frenchman who speaks English like a native, he has a razor-sharp business mind and loves to save money. Philip would not even meet my movers. He wanted to use a cut-rate company and pick up some migrant workers off the street. I begged. I pleaded, but to no avail. The movers and their unskilled helpers took twice as long as predicted. Items were damaged as they got tossed into boxes by the day laborers who had no idea how to pack safely. I held my breath as they made their way up and down the 100+ steps to the front door of the house. Did my client save money? Not in the long run, but he was delighted he had scored a "deal." If someone gives you a really low bid, you had best be sure they can fill the order.

PREPARING FOR MOVING DAY

Let's assume that the next location has already been chosen. I'd like you to take a piece of paper and divide it into two columns. Let's use the standard $8\frac{1}{2} \times 11$ so we have adequate room to write. On the left please list every room in your current residence. In the second column, please list every room in the new location.

For example:

Old Residence	**New Residence**
Kitchen	Kitchen
Bathroom	Bathroom: Master
Bedroom: Master	Bathroom: Guest
Bedroom: Child	Bedroom: Master
Den	Bedroom: Child
Dining room	Bedroom: Guest
	Den
	Dining room

Some rooms will be the same in the new location. For example, you probably have a kitchen, master bath, and dining area or room in both locations. You can list these rooms across from each other.

When the movers are packing up your belongings, it's a "no-brainer" how to label the boxes. You want your kitchen items to be transferred to the new kitchen, not the garage.

The sticky part comes when you realize that the contents of one room are going to a completely different room. Let's say, for example, that in your current home you have a den. The occasional guest has always slept on the sofa in that room. Your new home comes with a bonus: a separate guest room in addition to a den! If you want all the items in your current den to go to the new guest room, you need to be sure the movers label the boxes for the room the items are *going to* rather than the room in which they currently reside. In other words, your movers walk into your den and look around. They ask: "Is this your den?" "Yes," you reply rushing around on moving day like the proverbial chicken with its head cut off. At the new house, the movers take all the furniture and boxes to your new den when in fact you wanted all those items to go to the guest room. Now do you see how this works?

There is another way to ensure the easy transfer of items to their new location. Pick up some different-colored dot stickers at your local discount or stationery store. Be sure to get large dots— you don't want your movers to need a magnifying glass to see them. Designate a color for each of the rooms. I generate signs for my movers and tack them on the doors. I use standard $8^{1}/_{2} \times 11$ sheets of paper. The notes might look something like this:

MOVER ALERT!

Please label the contents of this room "Guest Room."

Kindly attach a green dot to each box.

(show a large green dot)

Now flash forward in time. You arrive at the new location a few hours before your movers. The obvious rooms like the kitchen need no explanation. All boxes marked "Kitchen" are being transferred from the old to the new kitchen. Outside the less obvious rooms, however, you are now going to post another Mover Alert. It might look something like this:

MOVER ALERT!

This is the "Guest Room."

Please bring all boxes with green dots to this room.

(show a large green dot)

Now your movers don't have to stop and ask you about the destination of every box and piece of furniture that enters the home. This takes time and drains everybody's energy. Don't forget to attach an appropriate color dot to your Mover Alerts when necessary.

If you are splitting the furniture in a room, be sure to create a separate label. For example, if the day bed is going to the new den because a real bed has been ordered for the guest room, you would attach a note to the bed indicating it is an exception and has a separate destination. At the new location, you might add a sentence to the Mover Alert for the den: "Please be sure the day bed from the old den is put in this room."

Does this take time and energy? Yes, but it saves you in the long run. Movers are not mind readers. The easier you make it for the men and women who do this difficult job, the more you save in the long run. You also have to explain what you want moved. I have seen movers take garbage from the kitchen and full ashtrays to a new location. Their job is to transport items, not to figure out the puzzle of your home.

While we're talking about movers, let me say that it's really nice if you provide for the people helping you. Treat your movers with courtesy and respect, and you'll find that's how they treat your belongings. I always suggest the following to my clients:

◆   Set up a bathroom in each location that is okay for the movers to use. Provide toilet paper, soap, paper towels, and a trash can.

◆   Have coffee, juice, and donuts on hand in the morning.

◆   Offer to bring in pizza and sodas for lunch.

◆   Have bottles of water handy, especially if it's a hot day.

◆   Provide a break area where they can enjoy their meal. This can be as simple as a picnic table under a tree.

When someone treats you with respect, don't you appreciate his or her actions? Don't you feel moved to better serve them? Your movers are human beings who will respond in the same way. At the end of a long day, heavy boxes can slip out of tired hands. If you have created an atmosphere that suggests you appreciate them, I guarantee those tired hands will catch those falling boxes every time. And although it's a matter of choice and never expected, a tip for good service is a nice touch. Don't express your gratitude in your check because the workers might not ever see the money. Have some cash on hand to express your thanks. And, yes, the supervisor usually gets a bigger tip.

CASH OR CHECK?

Be sure you understand how your move is to be paid for (cashier's check, cash, credit card, or personal check). If you don't have the approved form of payment, the truck will not be unloaded!

MERGING HOUSEHOLDS

Now would be a good time to take out your current inventory list from Chapter 2. If you are just about to move and merge your possessions with someone else's, please sit down with both of your inventories at hand. Item by item decide what is going to be placed where in the new home. You don't need to have a professional floor plan on graph paper, you can just sketch out each room in the new house or apartment. With your inventories at hand, ask yourselves these questions:

- ◆ How do each of you envision the room being utilized?
- ◆ Which pieces of furniture from your separate households will be used to best advantage to create the look you seek?
- ◆ How will you disperse the furniture that does not fit in the new space? Will it be given to relatives to store? Are you willing to pay for storage space at a professional storage facility? Or can you donate it to a charity and enjoy a tax deduction?
- ◆ What about accessories? You don't need to bring extra lamps, rugs, and decorative items into a home.
- ◆ Decide what you'll do with duplicate stereo systems, appliances, and the like. Can you sell or give away the duplicate items or use them elsewhere in the house?

TRASH OR TREASURE?

Organizing a garage sale is a wonderful way to offload your duplicate and unwanted items. If you don't have enough items, have a combined-family sale in which everyone helps with the organizing details. Be sure to advertise in the newspaper, post flyers, attach price tags to each item, and have a supply of dollar bills and coins on hand for change.

If you each come into this adventure with complete households, you will have to make some tough decisions. Compromise and practicality are the watchwords for this phase of your plan. It's better to discover that you feel differently about your possessions while sitting quietly at a kitchen table than on moving day, when the atmosphere tends to be chaotic even under the best of circumstances. Let me give you three examples from my clients. These experiences might spark your own creative solutions.

WHOSE CHINA ARE WE USING?

I had a client who loved his everyday dishes. In fact, he was so attached to them, he assumed his bride would want to use them as well. She not only had her own everyday dishes, she had two young sons. Her future husband's dishes were extremely heavy. She was rightfully afraid the boys would damage or break them in short order. What to do? She placed some inexpensive plastic dishes in a low cupboard so the boys could grab them easily. She and her new husband ate off her everyday dishes. In a kitchen serving four people and two large dogs, dishes that are light and easy to handle were more practical. The husband's heavy dishes went to their mountain cabin, where they fit the décor perfectly!

This gentleman also had two large dining room tables. Bachelors frequently collect furniture without giving too much thought to how well it all works together. One of the tables was ready to be donated to charity. The other could have served the family well. His bride, however, had an entire dining room set. It made more sense to use her table, chair, and hutch. They not only matched, they were practically brand new. They gave one of his tables to a charity (and received a much-needed tax receipt) and gave the other to a friend.

WHERE DOES MY STUFF GO?

Another couple I helped lived in a tiny apartment in Chicago. Ben had lived in this apartment for many years; upon getting married, he was looking at sharing the space with his new wife, Susie. This was a very delicate situation because he had years of memories in the space while she needed to alter the environment to honor the fact that a fusion of lives was taking place. Let me say it helps to work with a decorator or a professional organizer in these sticky situations. No man or woman is likely to get angry with an outsider. They might, however, go ballistic if they perceive a request from their partner as a judgment or a demand.

In this case, in addition to the emotional issues that attend shaking up a space physically, we had very little space to work with! One thing I noticed was how his clothes, books, and CDs spilled all over the apartment. The first thing we did was to create more space by consolidating. Instead of five or six small and highly inadequate CD holders, we got an inexpensive six-shelf bookcase on which to stack the CDs. This freed up a lot of space in the small living room.

Next we had to work on the closet. Allow me to make a generalization here: Men rarely have any concept of how much space a woman needs for her clothing. The new husband had allotted his new wife a mere six inches on one hanging rod, almost no shelf space and a breath of room on the floor for her shoes. He wasn't selfish; he was clueless! I told him he had given her the space one would give an overnight guest, not a wife. Ben is a gentle, well-educated man who dearly loved his new wife. He got it. We set about re-organizing the closet so that both of them would feel at home. Here are the steps we took:

- ◆ We carefully went through Ben's clothing to see if some items could be discarded. This meant donating more than a bag of clothing to his favorite charity.

- ◆ His bathrobe was the large, terrycloth variety that really eats space in a closet. We installed two hooks on the back of the bathroom door. That way both Ben and Susie had easy access to their robes without sacrificing closet space.

- ◆ We sorted all of his clothing into categories—shirts, slacks, suits, etc.—and put them in one spot in the closet.

- ◆ A shoe rack was purchased for the floor of the closet.

- ◆ To make more room, some of the hanging items like T-shirts were folded and placed in his dresser.

- ◆ We gave Susie the hanging rod on the left side of the closet. Ben had the right side. And, yes, they shared the longest rod in the center of the closet.

- ◆ Because the bedroom had no space for a second dresser, we purchased a portable unit with multiple shelves on wheels. This became Susie's dresser.

- ◆ We cleared off the shelves in the closet. On the top we put Ben's memorabilia. The second was divided into two and each of them had a specific area to store personal, everyday items.

- ◆ We moved seasonal items to the hall closet. You don't need your winter hats and gloves in the summer, or tank tops and flip-flops in the winter!

This portable unit serves as a dresser.

TO ANTIQUE OR NOT TO ANTIQUE ...

My third example shows how practical and emotional considerations can sometimes blind us to the feelings of others. Zoe had inherited an unusually large collection of high quality antique furniture. It was worth a small fortune. More than any monetary consideration, however, Zoe loved this furniture because she had grown up with it. Living with it reminded her of her childhood and her parents. She hoped to leave it to her children one day. There was only one fly in the ointment. Her husband Harry hated it all!

Zoe had sold some of the furniture, but the bulk remained. She felt that it would be impractical to sell this furniture and buy new things because the quality could not be matched. I am sure you can see how Zoe felt. I asked her some simple questions: "Imagine for a minute that this furniture belongs to your husband. It is you who have no attachment to it. How would you feel walking into a house every day that reflected none of your interests or tastes? Would you feel welcome? Would you feel loved and appreciated by your partner? Or would you feel like you were playing second fiddle to inanimate objects?" Zoe understood. The family room was cleared and designated as the room the family would decorate together. Several formal pieces of furniture were put into quality storage. One day Zoe hopes her children will want to take these pieces into their own homes. In the meantime, her spouse has at least one room to relax in that reflects his interests and personal style.

By the way, let me put in a word here about off-site storage. The best facilities are privately run and owned. My favorite mover, for example, has a storage warehouse at his office. You need an appointment to access your things. In addition, an employee always accompanies you. The facility is so clean you could eat off the floor ... much like in my mother's house! This is the type facility Zoe needed for her precious antiques.

In the world of public storage, you run the risk of other tenants coming by and breaking the lock on your unit. Some of the units do not have walls that go to the ceiling so a limber thief can simply jump into your spot from a neighboring one. The sites are so large, you can't control the cleanliness of the other tenants or what they choose to store. In large cities like New York, Chicago, and Los Angeles, rats and bugs can be a bigger problem than security. It's best to rent in a high rent district. For example, here in Los Angeles, there is a world of difference between the storage facilities in Malibu and those in Hollywood.

If you need off-site storage and have the property, try purchasing one of the portable storage units that large department and home stores sell. If you are blessed with a garage, hang up items like bicycles and add a loft for storage. If all else fails, ask a friend or neighbor if they'd like to make some extra money and rent their garage to you. Remember, no matter what solution suits you, you must keep your unit organized. Be sure and make the contents of the unit part of your household inventory list.

THE MOVING JOURNAL

One of the great gifts of the Internet is the plethora of information that is available to us. Why not begin researching your new neighborhood long before the moving truck arrives? This is especially helpful if young children and teenagers are involved. You can make them aware of activities and interests in the new location. You might want to keep this information in a large binder. In fact, why not keep your household inventory and your worksheets there as well? You can use handy index dividers to create separate sections. Create four sections and sub-divide information under them. I would suggest the following categories:

◆ **Preparation.** Inventories, worksheets, moving booklets and pamphlets (if you collect these), moving contract, etc.

◆ **Travel plans.** Tickets, hotel reservations, driving directions, etc.

◆ **New neighborhood.** Schools, restaurants, social activities, etc. Your real estate person, if you are working with one, is also a great source of information for these categories.

◆ **New home.** Utilities/cable, rental agreement or house purchase papers, gardening services (if applicable), waste removal/city garbage, etc.

You might want to use heavy-duty sheet protectors in the binder as well. I like this for two reasons: Everything stays fresh and clean, which makes using the binder an inviting experience rather than a chore, and you won't have things constantly falling out of the binder every time you pick it up. We tend not to use items that are annoying no matter how much helpful information they hold.

By the way, for a small amount of money you can pick up a label maker at your local stationery store. Later we'll see how this inexpensive tool can be used all over your home to create a sense of order. Let's begin using it here to make the label for the binder. Label makers all use cassettes that supply the tape for the labels. I would not use this machine to make labels for your boxes. It will be too costly. A Sharpie and careful penmanship are best suited to that task.

MOVING DAY

The nicest people in the world are likely to become a bit cranky on moving day. It goes with the territory. The following tips will help you gain control. It begins with some things to do the night before. If at all possible, enlist the help of some good friends or have your professional organizer orchestrate the event with the movers. It's a difficult experience to watch strangers pack up and move your private world. If you have chosen your crew carefully, you can trust you are in good hands.

ENLISTING HELP

It's wonderful if friends can assist you on moving day, especially with the task of unpacking. However, it is critical that you have a plan and they follow your instructions! A group of well-meaning people with no guidance is going to create more chaos.

Here are some tips to make moving day a little easier:

◆ Be sure to pack an overnight bag for all family members. It is unlikely that any room will be completely unpacked the first night. If everyone has access to their everyday items including soap, toothpaste, something to sleep in, a change of clothes for the morning, and a towel, they should feel welcome in the new surroundings. If you have pets, include pet food, favorite toys, litter, and litter boxes.

◆ Ask the movers to load the dress packs on the truck last. These boxes are very expensive. If you can get your clothes out of them by the time the truck is ready to leave, you can give them back to the movers and deduct their cost from the total.

◆ Don't forget to have the bathroom set up for the movers and have their food needs covered.

◆ Be sure to have cash on hand for tips and emergency purchases. Also remember to have your payment for the moving company available.

◆ If you have pets, keep them in a separate room if possible (such as an unused bathroom), away from all the hustle and bustle. Be sure to tell the movers about them, and put a "Do Not Open—Pets Inside" note on the door so the movers don't inadvertently let them outside. Put a few toys, bedding, food and water, and litter box in the room with them. Or take your pets to a friend's house on moving day. Moving is stressful for animals, too!

◆ Decide which rooms should be unpacked first. My preference is to unpack the clothing while my assistants work on the kitchen and the bathrooms. They get all items out of boxes so that it's easier for me to organize the cupboards and drawers.

◆ Assign friends to these rooms and ask that they work in the order set. You might want to do something other than the suggested clothing, kitchen, and bathroom order that I traditionally use. Just be sure you make logical choices based on your situation and that everyone involved respects your wishes. Too many cooks can indeed spoil the broth.

◆ It helps when you are unpacking if you can move quickly. I like to have one of my assistants come by every two hours or so and check the wrapping paper to be sure I didn't toss anything valuable out by mistake. The next thing my assistants do is cut down the boxes and stack them outside. (Be sure to have plenty of box cutters available.) Clearing the space at regular intervals will prevent you from feeling overwhelmed. This is a great task for any teenagers in the home!

◆ Keep fresh bedding for each person in a separate box that you can transport by car or that can be put on the truck last. Once the movers set up your beds, you will be able to dress them and sleep on clean sheets the first night.

◆ You probably won't be cooking for a few days but do make a special kitchen box that also gets put on the truck with the last boxes. If you need coffee first thing in the morning, you're going to feel much more welcome in your own home if the supplies are handy.

◆ Have heavy-duty garbage bags on hand for the wrapping paper. Most city garbage pickup will take your boxes if they are cut, stacked by size and neatly tied. Your wrapping paper is best taken away in bags. Again you want a large sturdy bag to make the task easier.

◆ If you have decided to paint any rooms or replace carpet, try to do this before your possessions arrive. These activities send dirt and debris everywhere. It's easiest to accomplish good results in an empty home.

◆ Be sure your new home is thoroughly cleaned before your arrival! You can always have a touch-up done when the movers are gone. It's demoralizing to enter your new home and find that key rooms like the bathroom and kitchen are filthy.

◆ If you work better with music playing, have a boom box ready!

SUPPLY CHECKLIST

Here are the products we have considered throughout this chapter. You might not need everything listed here; just check off what you need for your situation:

❑ Heavy tape, with a tape dispenser/handle (having two available makes packing go quicker)

❑ Boxes

❏ Scissors

❏ Wrapping paper (buy the white paper—don't use old news-paper, as it leaves print on your belongings)

❏ Bubble wrap

❏ Label maker and extra cassettes

❏ Box cutters

❏ Plain paper for making signs

❏ Different-colored dots for marking boxes and furniture

❏ Binder (two-inch width is a good size)

❏ Sheet protectors

❏ Sharpies/markers

ONE ROOM AT A TIME

If you are sitting in a new home, still living out of boxes weeks after the official move day, take heart. You can implement a personalized version of this chapter to suit your needs. Moving day is behind you. Your worst problem is probably that you have too many things in the space, right? You have run out of space and out of personal steam in the unpacking process. This is not an insurmountable problem.

You'll need to work one room at a time. Again, a functioning kitchen and organized bathrooms are the first places to start. Keep your goals small and achievable. "I need to unpack this house once and for all" will probably leave you feeling exhausted. "I need to set up my pantry" isn't as daunting a task. One small task at a time will take you to your goal of an unpacked and organized home. Your personal inventories will assist you as well. The elimination process will have to be implemented. And remember: The worst is over. You are already home!

FINAL NOTE

Most people have no idea how much they own. Over time, stuff collects. We put things on closet shelves, behind doors, in attics, under our beds, and into garages. We hope that one day we'll sort it all out. We are oddly comforted by the collection. The sheer size of it makes us feel prosperous. Many of us are convinced that among the trash are valuable treasures.

Moving can be a powerful catalyst for change. It will offer you opportunities to confront yourself on many levels, not just the obvious physical. Instead of unconsciously hauling everything you both own to a new location, you can craft a logical step-by-step plan to move only what you truly need and want. When this journey is to a new home that will be shared with someone you love, it's especially important to bring only the items that bring you both pleasure and solace. Home is meant to be your sanctuary from the world. Like all true sanctuaries, it is a consciously created space. The many rewards you reap will make the work involved well worth the effort.

4

THE BEDROOMS

"He who wishes to see how the soul inhabits the body should look to see how that body uses its daily surroundings. If the dwelling is dirty and neglected, the body will be kept by its soul in the same condition, dirty and neglected."
—Leonardo da Vinci, Italian painter

No matter how perfectly decorated and organized your home is, responsibilities and demands on your time will encroach upon your personal haven. If we view our homes as places of refuge from the outside world, we can begin to see our bedrooms as the sanctuary we run to when we wish to escape the demands of our daily lives. After all, babies wail, children fight, teenagers squabble, the telephone rings, and the mailman delivers bills we'd rather not deal with. At day's end, it is important to be able to enter a room that relaxes us.

Are you thinking that for you the bedroom is not important because no one sees it but you and your family? Well, consider this: Your bedroom sets the tone for the beginning and the end of each day. It is the first room you see when you open your eyes in the morning. It is the last room you see when you close your eyes at night to sleep. I think that's pretty important, don't you? Let's repeat an exercise we did in an earlier chapter, only now we'll put a slightly different spin on it.

Please go into your bedroom and find a comfortable seat. Pretend that this is the first time you have ever been in this room. Please answer yes or no to the following questions:

◆ Is the bed unmade?

◆ Are the nightstands a jumble of miscellaneous items?

◆ Is there a difference between your nightstand and the one by your partner's side of the bed? (For example, is one side tidy and the other side a mess?)

◆ Are clothes draped over the furniture?

◆ Do you see shoes cast about the floor like orphans?

◆ Is anything stored under the bed?

◆ Are items strewn across the floor that belong elsewhere (toys, recent purchases from stores, books, etc.)?

◆ Do you have a mini entertainment center in the room?

◆ If so, are the VHSes, DVDs, and CDs unorganized?

◆ Is there a boom box perched on your dresser?

◆ Is there anything specific about your bedroom that bothers you?

◆ Is it hard to find things in your closet?

Please add the number of your "yes" responses. If the total is six or more, you are ready to turn your bedroom into a sanctuary. Don't panic! We're going to do this together. Let's take a minute to examine some of the questions in our quiz and see what we can learn from our responses.

THE TIDY BED

When people ask me to suggest good habits they should cultivate, I always top the list with "Make your bed every day." An unmade bed presents us with an image of chaos. It is as if yesterday's unfinished business has been dragged into today's landscape. It is a visual guaranteed to make us feel tired or even a little depressed. If your bed is not made, is there a legitimate reason? Let's consider a few possible responses:

- If you or your spouse are currently sick, you may not want to make your bed for a day or two because one of you will be spending extra time there. (As soon as you start to feel better, change the sheets!)

- If you and your partner work different shifts at work, one of you may literally be crawling into bed exhausted as the other is starting the workday.

- An emergency may have taken you out of the house this morning before you were able to do your everyday chores. Remember that an emergency is something along the lines of an unexpected phone call informing you that a relative has been taken to the hospital. It is not an emergency if you are habitually late in the morning because you do not plan your day.

Sometimes we unconsciously set a room into a state of advanced chaos because we have unfinished emotional business. Is this the case for you? Please take a minute to answer these questions in your journal.

1. When the room was decorated did you plan the décor with your partner (preferably using your household inventory lists)? Is it possible you keep the room chaotic as a way of "punishing" your partner for making you accept a decorative theme you do not like?

2. Are you using bed linens from previous marriages or relationships?

81

3. Is it time to change the mattress either due to age or involvement in previous relationships? You may not have considered the mattress or the bed linens as being remotely related to the state of your relationship. In feng shui, the Chinese art of placement, it is believed that physical items absorb the energy of those who use them. From an energy perspective, you may be going to bed with a "crowd!" (There's more on feng shui in Chapter 11.)

4. Does having a chaotic bedroom help you avoid being intimate?

It might be true that the bed has not been made regularly because you are not conscious of the visual impact an unmade bed has on your psyche. It is depressing to say the least. If you have experienced a death in the family, for example, your chaotic surroundings will only plunge you deeper into depression. Conversely, a tidy home will lift your spirits. You always have the choice of creating an environment that supports or sabotages your best efforts. An unmade bed is one of the key elements!

Let's look at some other reasons for that unmade bed. Perhaps you grew up in a home where making the bed was not significant. I would bet that once you experience the serenity of a made bed for several days, you will never return to your old ways. It is also highly likely that answering the previous questions in your journal will lead you down a path of discovery. You might be shocked to discover that the mundane tasks in life can quite easily be turned into weapons in the emotional and control wars most couples wage. Whatever the past cause for the unmade bed, start making the bed every morning. It should become an ingrained habit, like brushing your teeth and hair before you leave the house.

THE PARED-DOWN NIGHTSTAND

It is uncanny how messy most nightstands are. If the bed is habitually unmade and the nightstands have tiers of miscellaneous stuff tumbling onto the floor, getting in and out of bed will not be pleasurable. Indeed it will be a little like climbing in and out of a bunker. What should go on a nightstand? Well, for starters, it is ideal for visual balance and the convenience of the inhabitants, to have two matching pieces. It's also great if you can have a top surface, a tiny drawer and an open space. Most nightstands that are part of a bedroom set look like this. Here are some practical items you might want to keep within easy reach:

- One lamp
- Telephone
- Remote control (if applicable)
- Tumbler of water and a matching glass
- Book or a magazine you are currently reading
- Eyeglasses
- Your journal (inside the drawer) with a favorite pen
- Any prescription medicine you might need during the night
- If there is an activity you like to perform in bed, you might want to keep your tools in the drawer (I had a manicure or a pedicure in mind, but you are free to be creative.)

Do you have a huge stack of books by your bedside? Consider adding a small bookcase to the bedroom. In fact, as we'll discuss later, it's nice to organize a book collection by type. For example, I have my favorite spiritual books in my bedroom, books of general interest in my living room, and reference books in my office. An unmanageable stack of books can be an unconscious way of keeping us from ever reading any of them. Who wants to start moving and re-stacking books every night? This jumble might also be an unconscious signal to our partner that our main agenda in this room is reading rather than being emotionally or physically intimate.

If magazines are an issue with you, try to add some acrylic magazine holders to the bottom shelf of your new bookcase. You can decide how long you want to hold on to your magazines and keep the accepted number of issues in those containers. I would suggest the outside number of monthly magazines you hold on to would be 12 issues. When the new issue arrives, toss the oldest. Let's face it, if you didn't read the issue in question in a year, you probably aren't going to in the future.

Some people feel guilty if they have a magazine subscription and don't read every issue cover to cover. Other clients tell me they just know that something of value is hidden in those pages and they must read it cover to cover. Here are two tips that might alleviate your guilt. Do you ever go to a fancy coffee shop and spend $3 or $4 for a specialty drink? It probably takes you 15 minutes to consume, right? How much pleasure do you have to wring out of a magazine? Flip through the pages when each publication arrives. If you spend an interesting five minutes browsing through it, consider your subscription money well spent.

CLIP AND TOSS

Don't save piles of magazines because there are recipes, craft projects, and so forth that you think you might try later. Clip out what interests you and keep it in a recipe file, folder, or scrapbook. Then toss out the magazine!

When you become immobilized with guilt and feel sure that something of value is within those pages, remember that we live in a world of constantly changing information. The latest on any particular subject is at your fingertips when you go online. Trust that the universe is a generous and loving teacher always bringing you what you need to know.

Books and magazines illustrate a key tenet in organizing a nightstand: Keep it simple. If you subscribe to more frequently published magazines, decide on a respectable time frame for holding on to them as well. And don't forget, the oldest issue exits when the newest arrives.

Food in the bedroom is a matter of personal choice. I prefer not to watch TV or movies or eat in my bedroom. Those activities stimulate the brain. My goal is to relax. In ancient times, yogis taught that you should keep the place of meditation sacred to that task. After a while, the energy of the practice would build up and just being in that spot would help you get centered and calm. In much the same way, I think we need to dedicate the various rooms in our homes to specific activities. If the goal is to experience intimacy and peace in the bedroom, extraneous activities and piles of stuff will become unconscious barriers to fulfilling our stated purpose.

In the earlier quiz, I asked if there was a difference between the two nightstands in your bedroom. Very often you can tell who wields the power in the relationship just by looking at the nightstands. One side has a small table that can barely hold a lamp and the tower of books parked on the surface. Things are constantly falling onto the floor and making their way under the bed. The other side looks like the command station at NASA's Mission Control. It is a much larger piece of furniture with all the power tools in the room (the phone, the TV, a larger lamp, etc.). In addition, you will see evidence of this person's interests and hobbies.

If you are surprised to see such an imbalance in your bedroom, it's time to negotiate for a change in status. Suggest, for instance, that matching nightstands would not only be a nice visual effect, but would afford both of you more room for the things you like to have close by. If the telephone is going to live on your partner's side of the bed, perhaps you could become the guardian of the remote. Don't forget that physical placement merely mirrors back to us the unconscious structure of the relationship. Is there a deeper significance to this imbalance?

UNDER-THE-BED STORAGE

If you can help it, don't use the space under the bed for storage of any kind. This area is designed to be open space. The one exception would, of course, be a platform bed with drawers. It would be silly to have such a bed and then not make use of the drawers. In tiny bedrooms where space is at a premium, these drawers can take the place of a dresser.

If you absolutely must store items under the bed, at least keep them tidy and organized! There are heavy-duty plastic containers on wheels designed to slide easily under the bed. Don't forget to label the boxes clearly using that label maker you bought to help with your move (see Chapter 3). These under-bed containers can be where you store blankets or off-season clothing items. If you store woolen sweaters, add some cedar chips to keep the moths out. You don't want any unpleasant surprises in the fall when it comes time to unpack these treasures. In the fall when the woolens come out, you can store your summer tops and shorts there.

CLOTHING: IN SEARCH OF THE GOLDEN KEY

If you have clothing strewn about the bedroom furniture, items vanishing under the bed, and shoes decorating the landscape, I am going to guess that your closet is in disarray. Organizing a closet is one of my favorite activities. For me, the closet is more like a jigsaw puzzle than most other areas of the home. Once you get the hang of organizing a closet and avail yourself of the appropriate tools, you can relax and actually enjoy this project.

I am always interested in the story behind the clothing. Let me give you an example. As it happens, this story is also about a power struggle in the relationship. Power struggles reveal themselves all over the home. They are by no means confined to the nightstands. If your bedroom and closet are playing host to a sea of clothing items, you might want to begin by asking yourself what's going on emotionally that created this explosion in your physical world. It may not be a power struggle for you, but I guarantee something interesting will be revealed about the status of your relationship with your partner! This is what I call the Golden Key: the reason behind all those clothes you see everywhere. In the following example, the clothes were all tucked away in closets—and therein lay the problem.

George was a tall, handsome, open man with wonderful manners. I liked him instantly. He worked as a carpenter. His wardrobe mostly consisted of blue jeans and work shirts. He hadn't worn a suit in years. His wife, Jennie, was as closed and private as George was open. She was about to give birth to their first child.

Jennie had her clothes in every closet in the house. Not only had she usurped all of the closet space, she had commandeered every drawer and cupboard. George's few items of clothing had been relegated to a tiny closet in a spare bedroom. That room was now being transformed into the baby's room. I saw instantly that I had been thrust into the middle of a thorny problem. The lack of closet space represented something much more profound. There was, in fact, no room for George in this relationship.

POWER STRUGGLE

A professional organizer can solve the challenges presented by your space. However, sometimes there are underlying issues, which are best dealt with in another arena such as couples counseling.

At the suggestion of Jennie's mother-in-law, a longtime client of mine, I was invited over to help Jennie get organized. Jennie had been offended by this but had kept silent. When I arrived, though, it was clear that Jennie resented my being in her home. She would not let me be alone in any room with George. She said she was afraid I would force him to make decisions he would later regret.

As you may have gathered by now, I never force, coerce, or manipulate anyone to do what I think is best. I lead you to a place where the appropriate choices come from you—choices you can be at peace with and live with long after my car has pulled out of the driveway.

George and Jennie taught me many invaluable lessons that day. I never again worked with two people simultaneously. Inevitably, as one is ready to toss something, the other is encouraging them to hold on to it. It was certainly true of George and Jennie. She insisted he keep just about every item he was ready to eliminate. I also learned that day that every adult in the household must be in agreement that things need to be organized.

Jennie had control issues that played out through clothing. Closets and drawers were jammed with items that seemed to have been purchased solely to fill up the space. George was left with a problem. Not only did he currently have to exit the master suite and walk down the hall to the spare bedroom to get dressed, he would soon be trespassing on his own child's space. Babies grow up and it was only a matter of time before Jennie would be tossing George out of this closet as well. I tried to reason with Jennie. The fact that George was not welcome in his own home except perhaps to eat, pay bills, and sleep was lost on her. A hotel room would have been a more welcome venue for George than his own home.

This couple represents the extreme, and yet we can all learn from them. Jennie had some deep-seated issues that needed to be addressed in therapy. As you can see, the struggle for closet space may be greater than the need to install a new shelf or clothing rod. Did you relate to this story? Are you the unconscious bully in your home, dispensing closet space to your mate as if it was worth its weight in gold? How would you feel if you were treated in this manner? And if the shoe is on the other foot, what brought you to a relationship where you are made to feel your basic possessions are an intrusion on the family living space? If there are tinges of Jennie and George in your relationship with your partner, you may want to explore the issue in your journal.

SIMPLE STEPS TO AN ORGANIZED CLOSET

When I work with a new client and we are going to do the home *and* office, I prefer to start with the closet. This is the easiest place to get acquainted with the Magic Formula that you learned about in Chapter 2. We *eliminate* the items that are no longer being used. As we decide which items are staying, we will place them in *categories*. And finally, we'll see how to *organize* our categories so that the finished product is beautiful, functional and easy to maintain. Sound familiar? Once you have the closet under your belt, the rest of your living and working quarters will fall in line easily. The guidelines are the same for women's clothing and men's. The big difference is that women generally have more clothing. It usually takes very little time to whip a man's closet into shape.

STEP ONE: GET READY

If organizing your closet is a daunting task for you, it's important to put all the elements in place to make the project a success. Set aside at least five hours for this project, depending on the shape your closet is in. If you balk at the idea of setting aside so much time, remember that in life we generally succeed in direct proportion to the commitment we make to achieve our goals. If you want an organized closet that can help you save time and enjoy getting dressed, you need to show respect for your goal. Time is the critical component.

Be sure to have lots of fresh water and healthy snacks on hand. Some of my clients like to work with music playing in the background. I prefer silence.

STEP TWO: GO DOWN THE LINE

Don't start by taking everything out of the closet. Piles of clothing on the bed will simply be wrinkled garments by the time you are ready to put them back inside the closet. This is one of those choices we unconsciously make that ultimately sabotages our best efforts. There you are with the best intentions and, by the end of the day, you can't wear half your wardrobe because it's now wrinkled. You start to believe that this is proof positive that you cannot be organized. Funny how this works, isn't it?

You will want to begin at one end of your closet and work item by item down the line. Resist the temptation to look up and get side-tracked by the mess on the closet shelf. It will have your undivided attention soon enough. Don't look down and become depressed by the sea of shoes on the floor. They, too, will have the spotlight at the appropriate moment.

Eliminating what is no longer worn or needed is the first step in our Magic Formula. When nothing remains in the closet except what you love and wear, we'll create categories and organize them by color.

STEP THREE: DECIDE WHAT STAYS AND WHAT GOES

You must decide as you move down the line the fate of each item of clothing. Generally, I put items into four categories: items that are being kept, those that are being donated or given to others, those that are being tossed, and those that belong elsewhere in the home.

◆ The obvious items you wish to keep will stay in the closet. Once you have made a clean sweep, we will return to organize the items you are keeping. For now, keep moving.

◆ Some things can go to the charity of your choice. You will get a tax deduction and your clothing will get a new lease on life. This is one of those genuine win/win situations. Here in Los Angeles, I support a women's shelter. My clients love the idea of helping women in transition who need clothing and furniture. You may wish to do some research so that your donation is empowering a group you delight in helping. Have a box to put these items into while you work or place them in heavy-duty trash bags.

◆ You may want to give some things to a relative or friend. This particular solution poses a potential problem. You want to be able to take the garbage bags out at the end of the day to the trash. You want to make your charity drop-off within 24 hours. (If you work with a professional organizer, he or she will most likely take your items to a charity for you. I do this so the clothes do not magically find their way back into the closet the minute my car pulls out of the driveway!)

If you have relatives across town or even across the country, a potential drama ensues. Do you have the right box for mailing? When can you get to the post office? This is often another unconscious way we have of preventing our true progress. How? Those items you're giving away are more than likely to sit in a box in the middle of the closet or become a permanent fixture in your bedroom. In the worst-case scenario, they might just magically migrate back into your closet!

◆ There might be some worn, outdated, or personal items that you can toss out. (I discourage the donation of undergarments like bras, panties, nylons, etc.—most charities won't take these.) Have a separate box or bag handy for items to be thrown away.

If you have trouble deciding what to keep and what to discard, you may want to work with a professional organizer. You might be lucky enough to have a relative or friend who is particularly adept at making such decisions. They can guide you and show you how to do it with dispatch. The key element in learning how to eliminate clothing items is to judge their relevance to your life. You don't want to work with a bossy individual who will inflict their opinions on you. Again, this is how we short-circuit the process. You get your closet organized but you now second-guess your choices because you feel you were unduly influenced by whoever offered to assist you.

Here are some of the questions I ask a client when they hesitate over an article of clothing:

- When was the last time you wore this?
- Do you consciously know why you haven't worn it?
- Does it still fit?
- Are you keeping it because you think you might lose weight?
- Is an old relationship or the memory of a pleasant event attached to this item?

I don't operate using any "time rules." If, for example, tossing anything you haven't worn in six months, one year, or any other length of time you feel comfortable with, is of service to you, then by all means use this as your yardstick. I find it a little arbitrary. It's always much more interesting to get to the emotional heart of the matter. Let me give you an example from my own closet.

For a long time I had a pair of blue jeans hanging in my closet that were sentimental favorites. The time had long passed when I could pour myself into them. These jeans were the tiniest size I had ever worn. To compound matters, I was in love with someone I had hoped to marry when I purchased them. We had even worked on a video project in which I wore these jeans. I certainly had a lot of memories invested in a few yards of denim!

I clean out my closet once a year after the December holidays, just before we greet the New Year. One December about two years after the relationship ended (and long before I did this work for a living), I realized that the time in my life those jeans represented had long past. Moreover those jeans were powerless to make it return. The wonderful benefit that comes when you let go of things from your past is that you learn to embrace the present more fully. After all, we are creating "the good old days" in this present moment. See if you can discover any emotional attachments hanging in your closet.

By the way, as they're cleaning out the closet, women often create a large pile of clothing they feel they need to try on. I am always mystified by this turn of events. If you haven't worn something in so long that you no longer know if it fits, I can almost guarantee it is an item destined for the charity box.

MIRROR, MIRROR

Be sure you have at least one full-length mirror in the bedroom. It's a good idea to be able to check your outfit from head to toe before you head out the door. The full body view will also help you decide if something really still fits.

STEP FOUR: DO THE SHELVES AND FLOOR

Once you have completed all of the hanging items, it's time to do the shelves and then move on to the floor of the closet. The interesting thing about these areas is that they are frequently the final resting place for items other than clothing. It isn't unusual for me to see things like family albums, old tax returns and sports equipment in these areas instead of hats, gloves, sweaters, and the like. One lady had a very heavy box tucked into the corner of her closet floor. I always respectfully ask permission before I touch anything in the home. I wasn't expecting the answer I received. "Oh! That's my husband's first wife. They haven't scattered her ashes yet." This is the perfect example of an item that you do *not* want to encounter on a daily basis!

During this phase of the process, you will probably have some items that belong elsewhere in the house. Please set them aside. You can place the items you are keeping on your bed in categories. The most common are those just mentioned: hats, gloves, sweaters, and the like. Right about now, you may look around your bedroom and feel a bit overwhelmed. "It gets worse just before it gets better" is the motto I give to all of my clients. Actually, if you follow the instructions here, this bit of seeming chaos will ultimately reveal itself as the harbinger of the peace and order to come.

You can match up the shoes you are keeping and leave them in the closet for the moment. It's very helpful to organize your shoes by color as well. Once you have completed the closet, you will find that the repeating pattern of the colors in each category is very calming to the eye. In addition, you always know where something should be. If an item of clothing is missing, there should be only two logical places to look for it: the laundry hamper or the cleaners!

I like to organize the shoes by flats, low heels, then high heels. Stackable cedar shoe racks will store your shoes elegantly and protect them from moths. If you wear mostly heels, you may prefer the chrome type. The ultimate choice will be dictated by the types of shoes in your closet.

A cedar or chrome shoe rack organizes both heels and flat shoes.

I generally keep the exercise/play shoes separate. You may want to put your casual and dress shoes on some type of stackable rack. Your play shoes can perch on the wooden shoe rack or hang over the door in a canvas shoe bag. Canvas works much better than metal over-the-door shoe holders because it is roomier and supple. Please place the shoes that are being given to charity in a separate donation bag. (You don't want to get the clothing items you are donating dirty.)

An over-the-door canvas shoe bag takes up little space.

I have a famous actress client who loves to collect beautiful shoes. Her collection tops out at just over 100 pairs. There were so many shoeboxes, she couldn't remember what she had. Who could identify 100 boxes of shoes on sight? I find cardboard shoeboxes a visual blight in the closet. I solved the problem by purchasing acrylic shoeboxes for her. Not only would her collection stay clean, but she could see all her shoes at a glance. Naturally, I arranged them by color. Instead of an unsightly pile of shoeboxes in the corner of her closet, she now has a visual display that is almost as beautiful as her shoe collection.

By the way, I am counting on you to take a break when you need it. You might want to walk around the block or jump on your treadmill for about 10 minutes. This is exhausting work because these are emotional decisions you're making. I ask my clients to sit in a chair when I do their closets. I hold up each garment and ask them to decide its fate. Sometimes someone will say, "Oh! I can't sit, I am a hands-on person." I assure them that they will be exhausted and sleep like babies that evening. The next day I always receive a phone call asking me how I knew what would take place.

STEP FIVE: ORGANIZE, ORGANIZE, ORGANIZE

The best way to organize clothing is a twofold process. First you place all related items together. This way you will always know that your blouses, slacks, suits, dresses, and jeans are in one designated area of your closet. Next you organize these categories by color. Putting your clothes together by color will assist you when, for example, you're looking for your red blouse and black slacks and time is at a premium. There is only one place for every item you own to be located. I like to use this guide:

◆ White	◆ Pink/red
◆ Off-white	◆ Green
◆ Beige	◆ Yellow
◆ Brown	◆ Gray
◆ Blue	◆ Black
◆ Purple	

If you are really enjoying this process and want to take it a step further, you can organize within every color category. For example, place the white blouses in this manner: sleeveless, short sleeve, then long. Behind each solid color, place the patterns in that hue.

The actual placement of the various clothing categories depends on the space you have and what is logical. I had a busy executive who had three extensive wardrobes: one for business, one for casual play, and one for nighttime. I placed all his business clothes in one closet. In the morning, he didn't need to see his beach clothes or his nightclub garb. We treated casual and evening as separate but related items and they were housed in his other closet.

Here are some other tips for organizing the hanging area of your closet:

- ◆ Face all your clothing in the same direction.

- ◆ Use one type/color hanger (wood is my current favorite). Whatever you do, please get rid of the ugly wire hangers that come home with you from the cleaners. In addition to being unsightly, they can damage your garments. Many cleaners will recycle them.

- ◆ Remove clothing from the plastic bags that cleaners use. Those bags seal in the cleaning agents. You don't want to be breathing those into your lungs the next time you wear the item.

- ◆ If some items need to be covered (your evening wear or your summer whites), invest in canvas bags with see-through plastic sides. Your clothing is protected and you can maintain the color order of your closet using these.

- ◆ Fold as many items as you can to gain more hanging space. For instance, T-shirts can go in a dresser drawer.

- ◆ If possible, move your outerwear (winter coats, jackets, raincoats, and boots) to the hall closet by the front door. It is more convenient and will free space in your clothes closet.

STEP SIX: CREATE MORE SPACE

On your bed, you have the clothing items you need to store in your closet on the shelf. If you have only one shelf, take a minute to look at the space between your shelf and the ceiling. In most closets this is a cavernous space that can easily accommodate another shelf. On the new top shelf you can store out-of-season items. On the shelf above your clothes, you can store the everyday items of the current season.

You won't be surprised to learn that I line purses up by color and stack sweaters by color. To keep the sweaters from falling over, I use shelf dividers. If you have lots of fine woolen sweaters like cashmere, you might want to place one or two in individual sweater containers or bags. Your shelf dividers are equally helpful when you are dividing purses. If you want to finish off these shelves like a professional organizer, make labels and identify your items. See how handy that label maker is?

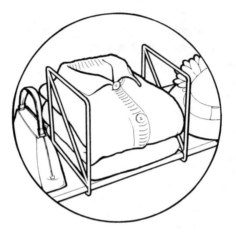

Shelf dividers come in handy in a closet.

Some items like soft winter hats, gloves, scarves, and mesh or link belts are best kept in containers. I like baskets that dip in front. They are called harvest baskets and were originally designed for use with produce. When you purchase your baskets, be sure to get the canvas liners that are sold with them (see the resources section at the end of this book for some stores that carry these and other items). This will protect your items from being scratched by the wicker. By the way, if you have been blessed with a hall closet, do transfer the baskets with hats and gloves to that shelf.

If you have ties and belts, the ideal solution is a rack that attaches to the wall. If wall space is nonexistent, see where else the rack could be attached. For example, you might have room for a second shoe rack on the floor for your sport shoes. The back of the closet door is now free and you can hang your ties and belts here. If neither of these are available as solutions and you have some hanging space, you can purchase a tie and belt holder that hangs on a rod.

A PLACE FOR EVERYTHING

A good rule of thumb is to keep every item you own in the area where it will be used. Hats and gloves are the final touches you need after your put on your coat. Keep them in the same closet if possible. Think of the steps you'll be saving each day.

DRESSERS AND DRAWERS

Whether you have an actual dresser, drawers under the bed, or a portable unit on wheels in your closet, you will have to have a place to organize your lingerie and sleepwear. I like to use modular plastic organizers for lingerie. They make various sizes specifically for socks, panties/boxers/briefs, and bras. You can also purchase containers in wood but the extra expense isn't necessary. It's a matter of choice and how much you are willing to invest. Using sachets is a lovely idea for women. You can seal your signature fragrance into your clothing.

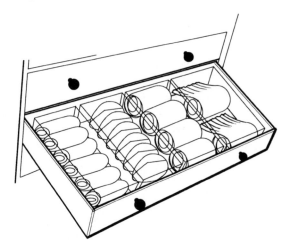

Underwear/sock drawer organizers keep everything sorted neatly.

Take a minute to sort your underwear and socks. Discard any items that are a bit tired. Arrange what you are keeping by (what else?) color. Fold your bras in half and tuck one cup into the other. Now line your bras up in the bra organizer. Voilà! You will never again have to sift through a jumble of cups and straps in search of a particular bra. Please do the same with panties.

I use plastic organizers for colored socks only. White sports socks are just too thick to be tucked into any kind of an organizer. (The exception, of course, is the person who has only one or two pairs!) You might want to keep them in a separate drawer; pairs together, of course. My preference is to lay them flat. Most people roll them into a ball. I feel this stretches out the top of the sock. It is totally a matter of personal taste.

In another drawer, place slips and nylons. Please check your washed nylons before you put them in the drawer. You don't want to be in a hurry one morning and discover as you dash out the door that your nylons have a run. If you have a lot of nylons and slips, you may need separate drawers for each category.

Finally, in the biggest drawers you have (traditionally the bottom) you may want to store your PJs and nightgowns. If you don't wear PJs and prefer to hang your nightgowns, you can use this deep drawer for your sweats. Again personal preference plays a part in how you get organized. For example, a corporate exec in a big city may have only one or two pairs of sweatpants and tops. They would fit nicely in this drawer and probably only be worn around the house on weekends. On the other hand, a stay-at-home mom will probably have a small wardrobe of sweat tops and bottoms. These could hang in her closet in a special sweats section or get stacked on a closet shelf.

Every closet I work with follows the general guidelines. I must also adjust the rules of the game to suit the individual needs of my clients and their lifestyles. You need to do this for yourself. This is why I say that getting organized is creative. You are always free to find solutions that are unique not only to your personality but to your clothing and accessory needs as well.

JEWELRY

Several years ago someone gave me a most interesting gift. It was a series of beautifully colored nesting boxes. I thought they were lovely but couldn't imagine any practical use for them. As I was about to toss them, I realized they would be great in the drawer where I kept my costume jewelry. I tossed the plain white store boxes the jewelry had come in and transferred everything to my new colorful boxes. Now my jewelry is not only sorted, the drawer itself is pretty! I think it's nice to store your costume jewelry in unopened boxes.

Of course, there isn't anything wrong with a beautiful jewelry box. If you prefer this, the dresser top is a nice place to have your jewelry box on display. Please do keep it tidy and organized. You want to open it and have your choices before you. Being confronted with earrings that have no matches, necklaces that are hopelessly tangled, and bracelets and pins that are broken can turn your good mood black in an instant.

There are also some clever acrylic jewelry holders in the market place. Each unit is dedicated to house a specific type of jewelry. There is one just for earrings and another for necklaces. One of my clients had a very clever solution for her jewelry. She moved her small dresser into her walk-in closet. On the wall space above the dresser, she placed a cork board. She hung her necklaces on push pins! Her large wooden jewelry box sat on top of the dresser.

My everyday jewelry choices are few. Like most women I am dedicated to the same old, same old when it comes to basic jewelry. I keep these in a beautiful box on my bathroom counter. When I finish my makeup, I put on my earrings and grab a watch. On special occasions, I open that dresser drawer and peer into my colorful storage boxes and have fun deciding which treasure I want to sport for the event I'm planning to attend.

If you have good quality jewelry, you should keep it in either a home safe or a secure hiding place (or keep it off site in a safe-deposit box). Buy a home safe that is either built into the wall or several hundred pounds. A tiny box from a stationery story is as easy for a thief to carry out as it is for you to bring in. You don't want to make it easy for a thief to get all the goods in one shot. Remember, too, that your best jewelry should be documented and insured.

WHAT AM I DOING HERE?

Every room in your home has a purpose. You wouldn't chop vegetables in the garage or change the oil in your car in the living room. Have you cluttered your bedroom with things that belong elsewhere in the house? Consider the following questions and write your replies in your journal.

1. What activities do you think should be performed in your bedroom (sleep, make love, read, meditate, etc.)?
2. What activities would you like to eliminate from the bedroom?
3. Why did you originally decide to perform these activities in the bedroom?

We frequently tell our partners that we want more intimacy. Often our words seem to fall on deaf ears. We might not realize that the physical environment we have created says, "Forget what I said. Intimacy is the last thing I want from you!" I hope this simple exercise sheds some light on this area if it is one of challenge for you.

How can you create more intimacy in your physical environment? Once the bedroom is organized and the closets are streamlined, you will feel better. This is a key initial step to take. Chaos creates a condition I call "brain dance." Our mental world is as jumbled as the physical world we live in. In fact, the mental creates the physical and then they proceed to feed off each other. Once you break this cycle of chaos with a little organizing, you will find increased mental clarity. Peace in the physical environment is a measure of the peace in one's soul.

Here are some fun things you can try to create a more intimate ambiance in your newly streamlined bedroom:

◆ Use romantic patterns and/or lush fabrics in your choice of bed linens, comforter cover or bedspread, shams, and throw pillows.

◆ Carefully choose the music you play in this room. Store your "bedroom music" here away from children and guests.

◆ Try a dimmer switch on your light to create a seductive atmosphere when appropriate.

◆ Burn candles on special occasions (just don't leave them unattended!).

◆ Choose romantic decorative items.

◆ Investigate the world of aromatherapy and create a sensual atmosphere.

DOUBLE-DUTY ROOMS

Because of space limitations, in many homes, the home office is set up in the bedroom. If you have no other choice but to conduct business in this room, it helps to shut off the area in some way. A lovely screen is helpful if you use the desk/computer at infrequent intervals. If, on the other hand, you use your home office area every day and moving a screen is going to annoy you, try to set the area apart by placing it in a corner and using an area rug. This is a wonderful way to create separate activity zones in any room. You might be amused to know that in addition to decorators, feng shui practitioners use rugs to indicate a change in the energetic setup of a room.

I once assisted a wonderful man who worked out of his home. Space was at a premium and so his office had to be in the living room. Ironically, he kept his filing cabinets in his bedroom. Imagine walking into your bedroom and the first thing you see are your business file cabinets! We moved everything related to his work into the living room.

We kept the file cabinets, his desk, and his bookcases against one wall. Even though the office setup now ran the length of the room, we created a psychological barrier. We turned the couch so that if you sat down to chat or watch TV, your back was automatically to the office. In addition, the office area was off the large rug that occupied the center of the living room. He was more at peace instantly in the room. And he would be saving time by not having to run to the bedroom for files.

FINAL NOTE

If you are not immediately comforted when you walk into your bedroom, take heart! Whatever you see, you created. As the architect of your physical world, you are all powerful to create something more calming, supportive, and intimate in its place. The obvious changes can take place quickly: Clear out the bedroom and organize the closets. The more subtle changes can evolve over time. It is here that you can have the fun of discovering as a couple what scents turn you on, what music comforts you, and what activities you wish to share in this most intimate room in the home.

5

THE KITCHEN

*"At feasts, remember that you
are entertaining two guests,
body and Soul. What you give to
the body you presently lose;
what you give to the Soul, you
keep forever."*

—*Epictetus, philosopher*

Most people would agree that the kitchen is the true heart of the home. We are drawn to this room because we unconsciously associate the kitchen with being nurtured. Food, after all, is key to our very existence. It is meant to be fuel for our bodies. It is the vehicle that brings the family together for the first and last meals of the day. It is the element we all look forward to on big holidays.

The main problem I see in the kitchens I organize is that no rhyme or reason exists in the way they are put together. On move-in day, people seem to be in such a hurry to empty boxes, they don't take the time to craft a logical setup for the room. Some things land in traditional positions. We all know that the glasses and dishes will be found near the kitchen sink. The pots and pans will generally be located near the stove. After that, it's a free-for-all. Let's see if we can't get a handle on the logical placement of items in your kitchen. In addition, we're going to look at several related areas including the pantry, the dining room hutch or sideboard, and the kitchen island.

WHAT'S HAPPENING IN THE KITCHEN?

Kitchens come in all shapes and sizes. I remember living in a studio apartment in New York that was so tiny, the "kitchen" was composed of a stove, a sink, and a refrigerator hidden behind a folding door. It was the kind of living arrangement only a 20-something would tolerate. As a professional organizer, I have been in kitchens that were larger than that studio apartment! What a joy it must be to cook and bake in a large kitchen filled with every convenience. Before we can start organizing, we need to decide what we're doing in this room and what tools we'll need. As a way of illustration, let me tell you the story of Steve and Lilly.

This young couple live in a two-bedroom apartment in Greenwich Village in New York City. Their kitchen is small by normal standards and huge by New York living standards. I asked Lilly if both she and Steve cooked. She assured me she was the cook in the family. As I opened her cupboards, I was amazed by the array of fancy cooking gadgets and tools she owned. Here I presumed I was a dedicated cook! Imagine my surprise when Lilly told me she only did the basics for her family. All of those gadgets were gifts from Steve's parents. These gifts were a double-edge sword: On one hand no one could deny the extreme generosity of Steve's parents. Every item was top of the line. On the other hand, no one could deny that it was ego rather than thoughtfulness that had been the impetus behind these gifts. With almost no counter space, Lilly would have no place to put a fancy mixer. There was no place to put an enormous ice-cream maker. You see the problem. The sea of unopened boxes seemed endless.

I suggested to Lilly that she ask her in-laws to store these gifts in their large home just outside New York City until Lilly and Steve either moved to a bigger apartment or to a house. They were contemplating a move in the next year or two. In their current living situation, these gifts were not going to be used. They were, however, filling strategic kitchen cupboards that Lilly desperately needed for her everyday needs. For example, the large cupboard that had been turned into a storage closet would make an ideal pantry for this family of four.

When I first entered the apartment, Lilly and Steve told me they did not have adequate kitchen space. In truth, although their kitchen was small, its major drawback was that it was filled with items they could not use in the present set-up.

Does this story shed any light on your current situation? No matter what size kitchen you have, please consider the following questions in your journal. This will give you an understanding of your situation before we start the organizing process.

1. Are there items in your kitchen that you cannot currently use?

2. Do you have things that you will never use?

3. Do you like to cook?

4. Does your spouse cook?

5. Do either of you like to bake?

6. Have you established a set location for the contents of your kitchen?

7. Are you both equally careful to return items to their designated location?

8. Are your countertops covered with school papers, mail, newspapers, magazines, and the like?

9. Do all your stove burners work?

10. Is the refrigerator covered in magnets, coupons, artwork, and papers?

11. Can you remember the last time you matched up your storage containers and lids?

12. Are there items in your kitchen you don't like or that don't work?

A QUESTION OF MINDFULNESS

You might have heard the word *mindfulness* discussed on TV or read about it in magazines or newspapers recently. It is an ancient concept from Eastern spiritual philosophies making its way into Western consciousness. What does it mean to be mindful? It means that you are fully invested in the present moment. More often than not, we are performing our household duties by rote. Inside, in the world of our thoughts and feelings, we are likely to be re-living something from the past or longing for the future. When you absently look at something and say to yourself, "I'll just put this here for now" you are almost guaranteed to forget the location. As we perfect our organizing skills, we want to make choices while fully vested in the present moment. As you learn to do this with organizing, you will find this way of thinking will spread to all areas of your life.

Our goal in this chapter is to mindfully create order in our kitchens. We want to shape this room and its contents so that everyone who enters this hearth of the home is nurtured on a deep level.

THE MIND/COOKING CONNECTION

Yogis believe that our state of mind affects the food we prepare. They never cook while angry or sorrowful, believing those powerful emotions taint the food. I often think of this when I eat out and for some unknown reason the food doesn't agree with me!

GETTING DOWN TO BASICS

Because kitchen sizes vary, as do the families making use of this room, you will need to adjust the suggestions in this chapter to suit your personal needs. The basics are pretty much the same, so let's tackle those first.

What does every kitchen have in common? Areas intended for specific activities. In fact, traditional kitchens are designed in a triangle using the stove, refrigerator, and sink as the major reference points of the triangle joined by counter space. Yours might not be set up this way but it will still be advantageous for you to establish activity zones. This is a fancy way of saying that we are going to categorize the tools and gadgets we keep in this room rather than let them live wherever they happen to be tossed. The most common activity zones are those dedicated to prep, cooking, baking, and food storage. Whatever size kitchen you have, think in terms of activity zones. We'll be returning to this topic later in the chapter; for now, let's look at some tips on organizing the things you use in your kitchen every day.

DISHES

Everyday dishes are usually stored in a cupboard to the left or the right of the kitchen sink. You can decide by asking yourself if you grab glasses or dishes more frequently during the course of a day. Now, are you left-handed or right-handed? See how easy it is? I grab dishes many times throughout the day. I have them to the left of my sink because I am a south paw and this is very natural for me. You want to set up every area to save you time and make you more comfortable. You can get more dishes in a cupboard if you use a dish stand. Not only will you be able to stack three sizes in one corner, you'll be able to grab what you need more easily. You can use more than one stand if you have a lot of dishes.

Most people have at least one set of good dishes. This is the set you got for your wedding or perhaps inherited from a relative.

Unless you have a very large kitchen with ample cupboards, you may want to store these in a hutch. Keeping a few pieces out for display will allow you to visually enjoy this set on a daily basis. I would suggest you store the rest in special padded holders. This helps prevent chipping and accidental breakage.

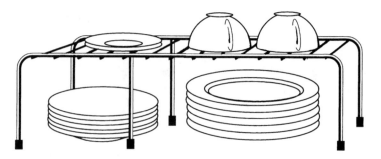

Store everyday dishes on a shelf.

KIDS' STUFF

If you have small children, you will want to create a space in the kitchen for their needs. As children grow and the desire to do for themselves increases, why not transfer some of their unbreakable dishes, cups, and/or paper supplies to a lower cupboard so that they can help themselves?

GLASS-FRONTED CUPBOARDS

Some kitchens come with cupboards with glass doors. This is a great place to put some of your beautiful items on display. You'll want these cupboards to be visually inviting every time you enter the kitchen. The sight of chaos will affect you by instantly jangling your nerves. A visually beautiful display will unconsciously make you happy to be in your kitchen.

DRAWERS

The contents of most kitchen and dining room drawers can be kept under control using small containers. In fact, these can be used all over the house to keep the contents of drawers organized. Instead of having 10 batteries in your kitchen junk drawer, for example, rolling wildly like dice on a crap table in Vegas, you'll have them in one contained area.

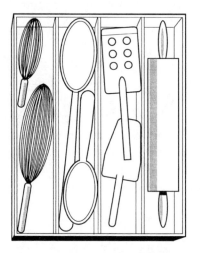

Keep miscellaneous items organized in kitchen drawers with sections.

And speaking of junk drawers, we all have at least one in the kitchen. Yours might be filled with things like tools, pens and pencils, receipts, chewing gum and/or candy, and those famous batteries. First we want to eliminate the clutter. One drawer for miscellaneous items is fine; two or more is excessive. You need your drawers for kitchen tools! After you eliminate what you don't need, put your categories into drawer containers.

SILVERWARE

Your everyday silverware should be kept in a cutlery tray. If you have extra pieces, you can store them in the same drawer by adding some separate drawer organizers. If you have fine silverware for special occasions, you will want to keep it wrapped and stored in your hutch or other place. There are special cloths designed for storing cutlery. You will need to keep silver polish on hand as well. A silver chest, if you have the space, is a nice touch.

SHELF LINER

I'm not a fan of contact paper, but if you are skillful at cutting and laying it in drawers and on shelves, by all means do so. I prefer the shelf and drawer liner that comes in a roll and looks like a thick paper towel. It grips the contents and keeps things in place. You'll find it in most kitchen supply departments. It comes in colors so you can be creative and use one color in the kitchen and another color in the bathrooms. See how much fun you can have? It's also washable and a snap to replace.

LABEL IT!

It's a good idea to label your shelves as you organize your kitchen. This way if you have teenagers in the home or if guests want to help you put things away after a party, they need only read the labels to know where things go.

SPICE SPACE

Spices grace just about every kitchen. How you store them really depends on how many you have and how often you use them. Spices retain their freshness for approximately six months; after that, it's best to replace them. No matter what storage option you choose, keeping them in alphabetical order makes it easier to find the spice you need. Be sure to check catalogs and home stores for ideas. New containers are being introduced into the marketplace every year.

Here are a few of my favorite storage solutions:

◆ If you have enough counter space, purchase a spice rack to display on your counter.

◆ Install a rack that fits under a cupboard.

◆ Install a spice rack above the stove (be sure the rack isn't too close to the heat from your oven).

◆ Keep spices in a deep drawer. There is a drawer insert you can purchase at most kitchen supply stores that will create levels for you in the drawer.

TOOLS AND SAFETY SUPPLIES

If you have a lot of tools, instead of cramming them into the drawers of your kitchen, why not invest in a toolbox? You can tuck it into the pantry if you are lucky enough to have one, or keep it in the garage. Either way, you won't have to walk too far to retrieve that treasured wrench when you need it. If you are an apartment dweller, try keeping your toolbox in the hall closet. (By the way, if your hall closet is a disaster, take heart. We're going to tackle that in a later chapter.)

It's a good idea to keep first-aid supplies in the kitchen as well as in the bathroom. If you burn yourself, you don't want to have to run to the bathroom for a Band-Aid and soothing ointment. You can keep an inexpensive fire extinguisher under the sink. They are compact and don't take up much room. Be sure to read the instructions when you first bring it home—you don't want to be fumbling with the extinguisher while a fire grows out of control in your kitchen!

THE REFRIGERATOR

Do you have a refrigerator covered with magnets? Are those magnets holding children's artwork, menus, coupons, and other assorted papers? Do you have Christmas card photos from years past tacked to your refrigerator? One or two magnets can be amusing, although I must say my preference is to keep the refrigerator clear. Some people cover the front and sides of the refrigerator with stuff. This is not only unsightly, I guarantee that brain dance is sure to engulf you the minute you walk into the kitchen. Keep this surface clean and post only what is absolutely necessary.

If you remind yourself of upcoming social events by posting the information on the refrigerator, try putting up a bulletin board instead, if wall space allows, and tacking up social engagements there. It would, of course, be best to note these events in your daily planner and put the invitations in a file. We'll develop this concept when we get to the home office in Chapter 10. We'll also address the use of bulletin boards and large calendars to keep track of your children's schedules in a later chapter.

HOLIDAY STUFF

We all have items that are used strictly during the holidays. The list traditionally includes a turkey roaster, special cookie cutter forms, a large ice-cream maker, perhaps some Easter baskets, and of course, lots of barbecue supplies. If you are blessed with a large kitchen and tons of storage options, this is probably not an issue for you. As you know by now, I like to keep related items in the same vicinity so having all of these items in the kitchen is ideal. These items might best be stored in a high cupboard you can't access easily. If you lack cupboard space but have an attic or a large garage, you have hit pay dirt. Be sure you store and label everything so it is easy to retrieve. Playing "what's in this box?" once a year is a waste of time.

If you don't have this option (think large city high-rises where space in general is at a premium), you might need to look at your apartment or condo and see how you can create special holiday storage areas. Do you remember the closet storage space we created in Chapter 4 by adding a shelf? Why not do that in the hall closet and use the top shelf for storage?

As a last resort for folks stuck with truly limited space, large apartment buildings frequently have additional storage in the basement or on individual floors. This might require an additional fee but might be your only option.

Sometimes we have tools left over from a time when we entertained large groups on holidays. If that time has passed for you, pass the turkey roaster and the holiday cookie cutters and the Easter baskets on to someone else in the family who now handles that tradition. The same can be said for barbecue supplies if you don't do much barbecuing. We all plunge into things at various times and purchase every possible accouterment. And then the moment passes. You need the space more than you need tools you used to haul out once a year.

After you eliminate what you can, if you find you still have items you need that will not fit into your kitchen, remember your dining room probably has a hutch and perhaps a sideboard. These are wonderful places to store holiday china, good crystal, and silver. If the room is large enough, you may be able to add a piece of furniture just for holiday serving items.

BIG-TICKET ITEMS

If you love to cook and spend a lot of time in the kitchen, it makes sense to have many larger, luxury items: the bread maker, the state-of-the-art coffeemaker, the juicer, the world-class food processor. The problem arises when you spare no expense, buy the best, then never use the equipment. Items sit on kitchen counters like trophies. It's a sad waste of money and space.

Still others purchase a big-ticket item before they are sure they have a place to house it. I remember going to one client's home and finding a huge box in the middle of the kitchen floor. When I opened it, I discovered one of the largest ice-cream makers on the market. My client had absolutely no available space, yet insisted that his new toy be on display. I cleared off the top of the refrigerator and voilà!

The toy was indeed on display. To date, more than a year later, it has never been used.

What's the solution? Ask yourself these questions when considering whether to make a large and expensive kitchen gadget purchase:

◆ Is this an emotional decision or do you plan on using the item?

◆ Can you easily afford it?

◆ If not, do you have other equipment that will perform the same tasks until you have saved enough money? A large food processor will certainly grind, cut, and blend everything. If you only need to chop nuts, however, for cookies, you can make do with a small hand chopper until you can either afford the top-of-the-line machine or create the space for one by renovating or moving.

Remember there are lower-end items that do a similar job and won't break your bank. I have a tiny cappuccino maker because I have no real counter space. It lives in a cupboard until I entertain. I have a client, on the other hand, with a huge kitchen. His state-of-the-art, professional-quality coffee maker is on display at all times. The bottom line is we both enjoy good coffee when we want it. Our solutions were based on space availability and finances. Yours should be as well.

◆ Where will this item be stored? Have you cleared a place on the counter because it will be used daily? Or is there space in a cabinet or on a kitchen island to house it when it is not needed? Have this mapped out before the item arrives.

ACTIVITY ZONES

Many of you will have your kitchen needs met by perusing the previous sections on organizing the kitchen items you use every day. But if your kitchen lacks an overall rhyme or reason, you need to think in terms of activity zones. Think for a minute about a famous surgeon you have read about. What if he or she was in the middle of operating on you and the head nurse suddenly announced that an instrument was not in the operating theater? She had forgotten to check her supplies before the operation. If you were in a twilight sleep and able to hear conversations in the OR, your heart would sink, wouldn't it?

Well, it isn't life or death, of course, but every day you may be wasting time in your kitchen simply because its contents have been tossed together without much thought. Why not avoid the frustration and anger by setting up the space to support you? Let's start by making a list of the most common activity zones in the kitchen. We will look at the organization of each. The key here will be to agree with your partner not only on the actual zones but also on what items are contained in each. Once you are in agreement, it will be easier to keep the cardinal rule of organizing: Keep putting items back where they belong! If you and your spouse both like to cook, you may want to have a discussion first about specific locations. If only one of you is the main cook, be sure to make the decisions logical, label when possible, and give your partner a tour when the job is done. Are you ready? Here are the most common work zones needed in every kitchen (as you'll see, some are related in function):

◆ Cooking

◆ Food prep/table setting

◆ Baking

◆ The pantry/food storage

◆ Cleanup

◆ Countertops

◆ The kitchen island

If you like to cook, you probably have a lot of kitchen gadgets. Where are you going to place them? The two questions you need to ask yourself about every item you use to prepare food are these: Do I use this item frequently or rarely? Are there items related in the kitchen? You had best keep them together. Let's take a look.

COOKING

In this area, you want to have all of your pots and pans. Be sure to whittle your collection down to the cooking necessities, especially if space is at a premium. The traditional place to keep cooking utensils is by the stove. Some stoves come with a storage area on top and one underneath. The top area is best for items not affected by heat. I wouldn't, for example, store my candles here. This cupboard tends to be high up and shallow. I might tuck rarely used cooking items here.

In some kitchens, the area above the stove is a large, deep cupboard. My clients take advantage of this large cabinet space to house some serving items. We all have the good china serving pieces that will reside in the hutch or the sideboard. We all need, however, large casual party platters and bowls. If these aren't used regularly in your home but you do want them close at hand, this cupboard is an ideal place to store them. You can go to the kitchen supply area of your favorite store and look for a shelf that can be placed here. You will instantly have more than one level for storage. Remember, you can use these portable shelves in any cupboard where you have a cavernous space and lots of small items.

A HANDY KITCHEN HELPER

To reach the area above the stove, invest in an inexpensive step-stool. Look for one that folds up to no more than an inch wide so you can store it in a tight space in your kitchen, such as between the refrigerator and wall. Keep one handy in the master closet, too.

The storage area under your oven traditionally houses flat items that can be used in the oven, such as broiler pans and cookie sheets. I have known some people who where so strapped for space, they kept their frying pans in the main oven. If you have a double oven and mainly use the top and the burners, this can work. If, on the other hand, you do use the bottom oven frequently and must now haul out the frying pans every night, this is not very practical. (It can also be dangerous, if you forget the pans are in there and turn on the oven.) By the way, I cannot lie. A hanging pot rack over a stove or a kitchen island makes my heart quiver in delight! It's a storage option that looks great, too.

If you have low cabinets on either side of your stove, you can keep your pots and pans there. Today, most kitchens come with drawers that slide out from cabinets. If you are designing or remodeling, be sure and take advantage. It will end forever the time you have spent sitting on the floor peering into the back reaches of your cupboards. This is ideal because when you need a pot you will grab a complete set. Time is wasted if your pots live in one area and the lids are scattered in another. If you must stack your pots, try to keep the lids nearby. There are containers that hold the lids in a row. You can also get some holders that will attach to the back of the cupboard door. If the sliding drawer is not available to you, measure this cabinet and see if you have space for a shelf. You can purchase a portable stand and have two levels for your pots!

On either side of the stove, we generally find some drawers. This is the area to store your potholders. The utensils that are most frequently used—wooden spoons, ladles, etc.—can sit on or near the stove in a caddy. I have mine in a beautiful pitcher. They can also be placed in these drawers. I like to employ drawer dividers. As you sort the contents of the drawer, you will probably be amazed to find you have multiple tools in your possession. Everyone seems to have lost track of how many nutcrackers, wine openers, and garlic presses they have! In the kitchen supply area, you will find these small drawer containers in plastic, acrylic, and wood. Remember how individual containers brought order to your lingerie drawers in Chapter 4? These will perform a similar magic here. In fact, you can use drawer containers in every room in the house. I like to line the drawer with a heavy liner so the contents can't go flying every time the drawer is closed. This bit of effort will bring you peace and calm every time you open the drawer in quest of a tool!

Unless you have an indoor grill, please don't store your grill tools in these drawers. They are of necessity extremely long and take up so much room. Pack them up when summer ends and store them in the garage or hall closet. Or perhaps you entertain weekly or have a large family and so you need your platters close at hand. If the cabinet on top of the oven is waiting for you to utilize it, perhaps the barbecue tools can live there? Remember, we're trying to be practical and creative at the same time.

FOOD PREP/TABLE SETTING

Stop and take a moment to list the items you habitually use to prepare your meals. I would make a double column. On one side, please list tools like your salad spinner or measuring cups. On the other side, list the kitchen equipment you use. Here is my list, as an example:

Prep Tools	Prep Equipment
Salad spinner	Food processor
Measuring cups	Blender
Measuring spoons	Mixer (hand and electric)
Knives	
Cutting board	
Colander	
Mixing bowls	
Wooden spoon	
Spatula	

Depending on your skill as a cook and the size of your family, your lists might be much longer or shorter than mine. Gather these items together. You will want to have them near the sink, probably in lower cabinets. The sink is important in the equation because you will be washing as you go. (Yes, I really did say that!) Some of your equipment can sit on the counter if there is enough space. If you use your food processor every day, it would be a waste of time to haul it out every evening before dinner. Try to keep any equipment you use regularly out and clustered in one area. Didn't it make sense to keep all your shoes, blouses, and slacks together in the closet? This is another grouping, only the items are different in character. We will use this principle throughout the house.

A word of caution: Don't haul out all your equipment and place it prominently on your counters. If you have, for example, a sandwich grill, waffle maker, bread maker, and pasta machine, these are probably weekend tools at best that should be stored out of sight—perhaps near the sink in the cabinets designated as prep. When you decide you need one of these items, there will be only one area to search.

In my list of everyday items, you might note I have some small items like a wooden spoon and knives. I store most of my tools in drawers near the sink. I do, however, keep the spatulas, wooden spoons, and whisks in the pitcher I mentioned earlier. If you have a large array of knives, a wooden knife holder on the counter is a great way to display them. The only exception is a home with very young children. Be sure to keep all sharp objects out of their reach.

Once the food is in the oven or simmering on the stove, you'll want to set the table. If there are children in the home, this is a great chore for them. Keep all the items you need nearby. For example, keep the tablecloth or placemats and your napkins near your kitchen table. Don't waste steps walking in the opposite direction of the table to get these items. You can grab your silverware each evening or keep it with some napkins on the table in a pretty pitcher. Good linens are usually stored in the hutch. The napkins and silverware slip into the small drawers while the tablecloths can be placed in the large bottom drawer. If you like to keep your linens hanging on the dry cleaner hanger, just be sure you have space in a nearby closet. Your solution will depend on the extent of your good linen collection.

BAKING

If you are an avid baker, you will want to keep your baking tools (muffin tins, cookie sheets, bundt pans, rolling pin, etc.) in one area. This will be close to the everyday food prep items but preferably in a separate cabinet or compartment. If you are an occasional baker, your stash of tools will be fewer in number and can be stored away from the daily activity zones in the kitchen. First, take an inventory of your baking tools to see what you have to contend with.

The important consideration here is that you don't want to have to sift through these baking tools when you need the salad spinner so you can prepare tonight's dinner salad. It's amazing how often we set up our physical spaces as if an obstacle course made our efforts more worthwhile. Save your energy for the task at hand. Set up your entire home to support your every effort. You will be amazed how nurtured and loved you will feel the minute you enter the front door.

THE PANTRY/FOOD STORAGE

Growing up in a Brooklyn brownstone, a separate pantry was a non-existent concept. In Los Angeles, just about every home has one, even if it's tiny. Let's talk first about a separate pantry. It is a thing of beauty, isn't it? A separate area just to store your food is a true gift. Guess what? You have all the concepts under your experience belt to set this space up in a logical manner.

First consider what categories you can divide your pantry food into, such as the following:

- ◆ Breakfast cereals
- ◆ Carbohydrates: rice, pasta, potatoes
- ◆ Canned soups

- Canned vegetables

- Canned meat and fish

- Flavor enhancers: oils, vinegars, marinades, etc.

- Desserts: pudding, cake mixes, candy, etc.

- Snacks: crackers, cookies, popcorn, etc.

- Baking/cooking items like flour and sugar

- Beverages: tea, coffee, canned or bottled juice, soda, bottled water, etc.

- Pet food (dry and canned)

- Paper goods: paper towels, paper plates, aluminum foil, etc.

BUG-FREE STORAGE

Many food items such as flour, sugar, pet kibble, dry cereals, and pasta are best stored in airtight containers to prevent bug infestation.

Beverages like soda and bottled water should be stored on the lower shelves or preferably on the floor under the last shelf. You don't want to risk bringing down a shelf under the weight of all that liquid!

I like to keep items like potatoes and onions in harvest baskets. Remember these from Chapter 4? We put belts, gloves, and caps into them in the closet. Now we see their intended use. In the closet you will want to use them with a liner; here it isn't a necessity. In the closet we used shelf dividers to separate sweaters; here we can use them to keep food categories separate. And of course, if it's possible, I just know you'll want to label these pantry shelves!

Cans are best stored on shelf creators. This way you won't have to pick up several cans to find the soup or the vegetable you want. They will be on raised levels and much easier to identify.

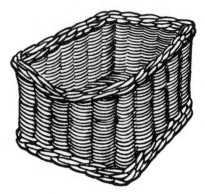

Harvest baskets serve many uses.

Shelf creators.

Finally, what does one do with all those packets of instant foods like soups and salad dressings? These can be placed into a square plastic container with a handle found in every kitchen or closet supply area in your favorite home store. They come in colors, but I prefer white. These will always be in stock! I place this container in the "flavor enhancer" section.

If you have not been blessed with a separate pantry, take heart. You will need to do one of two things: Use some cabinets in the kitchen proper and/or place a freestanding cabinet in the kitchen or just outside in the dining room. I know lots of families who keep the basics in the house and store backup food on shelves in the garage. We'll talk more about this when we come to garage organization.

CLEANUP

Everyone has their favorite selection of food storage items. There are disposable containers, Tupperware, plastic wrap, aluminum foil, large and small plastic bags, and so on. No matter what products please you, be sure to keep them together. It's nice, for example, to have all the wrap products like foil in one drawer. I like to keep one of everything in this drawer so I can see what I have and grab it easily. Try to keep your backup in the pantry or garage if you are lucky enough to have this at your disposal. When you have several boxes of foil or storage bags in one place, it's human nature that family members will have more than one open at a time. Isn't it frustrating to think you have a well-stocked stash of products only to have several boxes go empty at one time?

And now I must ask you to do something you probably dread. Yes, that's right, please sort your Tupperware and toss the "extra" pieces. I know you paid good money for it. I know you're certain that lid or bowl is going to turn up. In reality, this is usually a chaotic heap of plastic. Sort the containers you decide to keep. Keep the square shapes and the round shapes together. And don't save more than you need. Think it's a waste to toss items? It's a bigger waste to keep them. It wastes time to keep items that rob you of space for things you do use and steal minutes from your day when you want to grab just what you need. If you can't bear to throw them away, you might have a friend or family member who could use your castoffs.

COUNTERTOPS

Please take a minute to look at the items on your countertops. We have decided to keep out the cooking equipment you use on a daily (or close to it) basis. Now we need to survey the landscape and see what is still out. Do you need everything you see? Keep the items you use daily clustered in categories on the countertops. For example, the coffee maker and the toaster are a logical category and belong together. This makes breakfast easier to prepare. Just as clustering frequently used cooking gadgets makes meal prep a snap.

Some of my clients are absolute purists. They want everything put away. If you have the space to store everything and the energy to haul it out, this is a fine solution. Items on the counter are a matter of taste. Your kitchen might demand individual items be on display. For example, in most Italian homes you will find a beautiful container of olive oil out by the stove because it is used daily. Some of my clients keep butter out so that soft spread is always at their fingertips. Whatever you decide, remember that "lean and mean" isn't just a description of awesome abs!

Have your countertops turned into a mini office? Why not have a basket on the counter so the mail and any school papers can be dropped off as your family members enter? The basket, however, is just a holding tank. Each and every day, perhaps after dinner, the contents must be dispersed around the house. (I'll be addressing magazines, newspapers, children's homework, bills, and recipe organization in later chapters.) The bottom-line solution can be found in a friendly little saying my mother chanted every day like an ancient mantra: "There is a place for everything and everything should be in its place." Sometimes it's the obvious and simple solution that works best.

Speaking of simple solutions, do you waste time every day searching for your house and car keys? Why not put up a decorative hook or hooks by the entrance you use most often? As you race out to catch the bus or get in your car, your keys will be close at hand where you can always find them. Later, in Chapter 11, you'll see an illustration of a feng shui mirror hanging above a table in the entry. A basket on the table is another great place to hold keys. The important point here isn't the hook or basket, it's designating one area for your keys and honoring that decision.

Before we leave this section, let's consider cookbook storage. No matter how vast your collection, I am going to bet you rely on a chosen few to assist you in the kitchen. Please do keep these old friends on display. The counters, or even the top of the refrigerator, are ideal places. However, be sure you keep your cookbooks propped up with sturdy bookends. You don't want them falling all over the counter. It robs you of space and is visually distressing. If you have some wall space in the kitchen, consider adding a small bookcase for the overflow books.

THE KITCHEN ISLAND

Very few home kitchens are large enough for this helpful treasure. If you have some space in a corner, you can always keep a small portable island there and pull it near the sink at meal times. This is a great place to put everyday items if you lack counter space. Try to get an island with some drawers so you have more choices for everyday tools. And of course, you'll want a chopping surface.

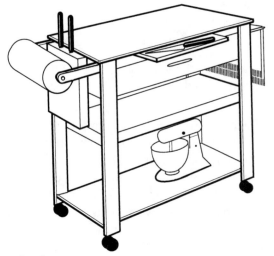

Kitchen island.

If you are lucky enough to have a large kitchen with a built-in island, hang your pots above it, if possible. The built-in islands generally have burners. I like islands with closed storage space underneath. This way everything stays cleaner. Whether you have open space or cupboards, be sure to keep the area tidy. Don't stack too many items in one spot just because they fit. Ideally, you want to reach and grab what you need immediately. Having to move and juggle items will once again not only waste time, it will make you irritable. Remember those yogis? You put into the food what you feel. You want to be organized so that cooking is a pleasure. Peace and joy will in turn be the secret ingredients in all your meals.

THE WORLD UNDER THE SINK

For some reason, this area is almost always a hotbed of chaos even in the most organized kitchens. Take heart, it doesn't have to be! Let's consider first what needs to be here. I would suggest the following:

◆ A fire extinguisher

◆ Box of garbage bags

◆ Cleaning supplies for the kitchen

If your kitchen is on the small side, you might need to use this area for other items as well, such as vases (not fancy or expensive!) or candles.

If you have a fairly good size under-the-sink area, you can actually divide it in half. On one side, you can stash your candles and everyday vases. On the other you can have your cleaning supplies. If you take the time to sort your cleaning products, you'll come up with categories. These can, in turn, be stored in those portable plastic containers with handles that we have used elsewhere. For example, your scrubbing powders and scouring pads are one category while your brass and silver polishes makes up another. We don't want to have to sift through oceans of products in quest of a sponge! It's equally important not to have products tossed under the sink without any rhyme or reason.

You may want to browse through catalogs and magazines to see the latest in under-sink storage. Recently I saw a clever shelf unit that fits around the drainage pipe. As with your quest for the perfect spice storage, investigate and use whatever method appeals to you and works with your particular situation. This is how getting organized can be fun!

CHILDPROOF YOUR CUPBOARDS

If toddlers are in the home, move all cleaning products from accessible areas such as under the sink to areas they can't reach until they are old enough to understand this is not a play zone. Or make sure the cupboard is kept locked.

FOOD SHOPPING/MEAL PLANNING

Once your kitchen is organized, you will find that you have a better handle on what you need at the grocery store. One couple I know hung a bulletin board in their kitchen. One side is cork in case they want to post a message. The other side is a chalkboard. Here they put the items they see they need at the store. As they exit, whoever is going to the store jots down the items needed and then erases them from the board.

If you are part of a large family, you might want to take a few minutes at the computer one day and log in a list of the general items you buy at the store. If you go to more than one store, list your items by store. You can check off what you need and generate a new shopping list each week. In addition, be sure to plan your meals in advance. Add the ingredients you'll need to your weekly list; this will save you last-minute dashes to the store to pick up a missing ingredient.

THE LAUNDRY ROOM

Frequently found just off the kitchen, let's consider the laundry room before we exit the chapter. If each bedroom has a hamper with a laundry bag inside, it can be brought to the laundry room when it's full. If space does not allow for a hamper, the laundry bag can be kept on a hook over a door in the closet or the bathroom. Now that each person is bringing down his or her dirty laundry, it's nice to make the task even easier. Organize your laundry products by category. You can keep the detergent, bleaches, stain removers, etc. grouped together. If you have them in a cupboard you might even (what else?) label the shelves.

If you have pets, the laundry room can be an ideal place to store their food should you not have a pantry. If you feed your pets dry kibble, be sure you empty it into airtight containers to keep out bugs. This will also ensure the freshness of the food. By the way, if ants become a problem, remember that they will not cross water. You can place your pet's food bowl in a slightly larger saucer (one from the plant store will do) and fill it with about $1/4$ inch water. Voilà! It is now safe from ant infestation.

THE ADVENTURES OF WILD BILL AND CALAMITY JANE

Many years ago I was called to the large home of a couple named Bill and Jane, who lived in one of the fabled gated communities of Los Angeles. From the street you couldn't tell that a treasure lay hidden behind the imposing iron gates. I was delighted to find a sprawling home with several buildings on a multi-acre plot. No expense or detail was overlooked in creating the perfect home. The kitchen was truly a design dream come true. Copper pots glistened above the stove on an exquisite rack. Every exotic spice known to man lived in the cupboards. The large pantry groaned under the weight of home staples. Still, there was a sense of this room being a movie set more than a working kitchen. I noticed, for example, that the new patina on the pots was barely worn. Also, I didn't spy any fresh produce.

I asked Jane who the cook in the family was. Sheepishly she said she liked to cook but it was her husband, Bill, who was the mainstay of the kitchen. Except for one small detail. The home was only a few months old and Bill had already refused to continue cooking until his wife made a change. Jane, you see, never, ever put anything back in the same place. Bill would spend hours organizing the kitchen only to have Jane destroy the order within a week. He had given up cooking in frustration. Every dish required a treasure hunt for ingredients and tools. Jane asked if I would please organize the kitchen. Sadly, I had to refuse.

Jane resented having to return items to a designated spot. I knew that she wouldn't honor order even if I labeled the shelves. She felt that her artistic side would be compromised by this kind of perceived rigidity. As a former actress and now a writer, I always assure my artist clients that order does not imprison their creativity. Rather, it frees it by setting a stage where true artistic license can flower.

I suggested to Jane that she and Bill might want to investigate some couples counseling to discover the underlying issues at work here. On the surface their kitchen was a playground of space and convenience. And yet, it could not be used without a struggle. Unfortunately, they decided against both therapy and an organized kitchen. I pass their community from time to time and always wonder what happened with Wild Bill and Calamity Jane's kitchen!

Right about now you might be sitting in a matchbox-size kitchen thinking of all the great things you could do in a kitchen like Jane and Bill's. Let me close this story by telling you about a friend of mine, Tanya, who is a caterer. Her food is exquisite. The taste and the presentation leave nothing to be desired. Tanya can cook for up to 200 in her kitchen—and it's the size of a glorified breadbox! She is a genius at utilizing not only a minimum number of cabinets but the adjacent space as well. When it comes to doing what we love, I think truly the motto that should guide us is: "Where there's a will, there's a way!"

CREATING A MORE INVITING SPACE

Once your kitchen is organized, you'll find you enjoy being there more. Why not make it an even more inviting place for your family? Try these simple touches:

◆ Place a bowl of fresh fruit on the table.

◆ Set some small plants on the windowsill (if you have the right exposure you can grow your own herbs).

◆ Bring home fresh flowers for the table once a week when you go shopping.

◆ Place a small lamp on the counter so the kitchen is filled with a more inviting atmosphere in the evenings. No counter space? Try putting the overhead light on a dimmer switch.

◆ Place a whimsical kitchen witch or a sacred icon like laughing Buddha on a shelf and ask to have the meals blessed.

FINAL NOTE

The kitchen is one of the most important rooms in the home. It is where we nurture our bodies. It is one of the key rooms we share as a family. Working and eating in a room that is a chaotic disaster will affect us emotionally. It is a complex room with many areas. There is no question it takes some time to organize. The rewards, however, far exceed the effort.

6

THE BATHROOMS AND LINEN CLOSET

"The soft overcomes the hard;
the slow overcomes the fast.
Let your workings remain a mystery;
just show people the results."
—*Lao Tzu, Chinese philosopher*

The bathroom frequently holds a secret. When I have been called to a home to organize it, I am always suspicious when the common rooms such as the living room appear pristine. Did my client pick up to impress me? Because I specifically ask that the home be left "as is," this is rarely the case. Most people are driven to make the areas of the home open to family and friends appear to be in perfect order. They imagine they will be judged on the level of chaos apparent in these rooms. When we go into the private areas such as bathrooms, I see a true explosion. It's as if what the world thinks is far more important than the reality we experience on a day-to-day basis.

I am particularly sensitive to this way of thinking because my own mother was a victim of its demands. A child of the Great Depression, she never left poverty behind her in her thoughts or her basic belief system. If someone was coming over to our home for dinner, for example, my mother literally engaged in an explosion of preparation akin to spring cleaning. But those bathroom cabinets, cupboards, and drawers continued to hide a private explosion. Are you like my mother?

Couples very often have to share a bathroom. It's so critical that all shared spaces are organized. There isn't any point in supplying a reason for an argument, is there? Whether you have a postage-size bathroom or a spacious one, let's see how you can create a *system* for organizing your "stuff."

A PRIVATE LANDSCAPE

Is your bathroom a chaotic battleground? Do you feel cramped and in need of more space? Do dirty towels habitually land on the floor? Is there a fragrant ooze from a soap dispenser spreading across the counter as you read this? Are you thinking that the bathroom isn't important because only you and your partner see it?

Your home should be the place where you are free to give full expression to your creativity. I believe that you are a spiritual being and getting organized is a way to show respect for yourself. Whatever you do in this life, your goals will be easier to achieve if you live in a calm, peace-filled environment. Each day of your life begins and ends with a visit to the bathroom. Let's see if we can't make this a sacred space that works in concert with the order we are creating throughout the home.

Why not begin with some work in your journal? Please take a minute and answer these questions.

1. Did you share a bathroom when you were growing up?
2. Whether alone or shared, what was the habitual condition of this room?
3. If shared, were you the neat sibling or the sloppy one?

4. Is your bathroom a mirror of your parent's bathroom or does its condition stand in stark contrast to what they experienced?

5. When you first left home, did you always keep a tidy bathroom?

6. If the answer is yes, is the bathroom where you now live still tidy?

7. If not, what caused the change? Is your spouse a bit sloppy, for instance? Or did you let things slip with the birth of your children?

8. Is there any possibility that unconsciously you have created the current situation as a deterrent to emotional or physical intimacy with your partner?

Most people think that a chaotic bathroom is the result of some outside influence. For example, you presume you live in chaos because you may not have adequate hooks, shelves, or cupboards. While those are certainly contributory factors, something deeper may be at work if you have let the situation fester. These journal questions might empower you to suddenly realize that you struggled with an older sibling for control of the bathroom and now your marriage mirrors that struggle. You might not have been conscious that the birth of a child caused you to be overwhelmed, for example. Even a joyous experience can be the beginning of your private world falling into disarray.

As I said earlier, the questions throughout this book are not meant to be magic talismans that will instantly springboard you into a new way of being. They may, in fact, bring home the need for some private counseling or counseling done with your partner. The main reason I ask them is to open the window of discovery for you. After all, if you do have some deeper issues lurking about, all the hooks and shelves in the world won't rescue you.

What do you do in your bathroom? Let's make a list:

◆ Cleanse the body

◆ Hair care routines

◆ Personal care rituals

◆ Store medicines

◆ Relax

◆ Read (you know who you are!)

Let's look at each of these and see how we can best organize the tools for each task, shall we?

WHAT'S IN *YOUR* BATHROOM?

As I write this, the bathroom of a client comes to mind. It is so large they put in a small refrigerator and a microwave. When they want to have a snack in bed, they have only to trundle into the master bath! If your bathroom is this size, your issue might not be one of space, but organizing what you have. For the rest of us, we need to learn how to maximize the space available to us. With this in mind, let's begin by taking an inventory of traditional bathroom supplies. I am going to leave some spaces for you to write in items that are specific to you. Feel free to cross off items that don't apply to you.

Cleansing products:

◆ Soap: soft/bar

◆ Body wash

◆ Shampoo/conditioner

◆ Toothpaste/toothbrush/floss/mouthwash

◆ _____

◆ _____

Hair care products:

◆ Hairspray

◆ Gels/mousse

◆ Barrettes/hair clips/bobby pins

◆ Scrunchies/ribbons

◆ Hair color products

◆ Brushes/combs

◆ Curlers

◆ Blow dryer

◆ Curling iron

◆ _____

◆ _____

Personal care:

◆ Beauty products (foundation, blush, eye shadows, eyebrow pencils, mascara, eyelash curler, tweezers, etc.)

◆ Razor

◆ Aftershave/shaving foam or gel

◆ Deodorant

◆ Feminine products (pads, tampons, etc.)

◆ Contact lens solutions

◆ Face/body lotions

◆ Face cleansers

◆ Nail products (polish, polish remover, emery boards, cuticle sticks, etc.)

◆ _____

◆ _____

Medications:

◆ Cold remedies

◆ Analgesics (aspirin, ibuprofen, etc.)

◆ Prescription drugs

◆ General first aid supplies (Band-Aids, gauze, tape, etc.)

- ◆ Special care (for example, diabetic or asthma supplies)
- ◆ Pregnancy-related materials (tests, thermometers, etc.)
- ◆ _____
- ◆ _____

Relaxation products:
- ◆ Aromatherapy products (oils, potpourri, etc.)
- ◆ Candles
- ◆ Bath products (bubble bath, bath pillow, powders, etc.)
- ◆ Sex-related items (lubricants, condoms, "toys," etc.)
- ◆ _____
- ◆ _____

Reading matter:
- ◆ Magazines
- ◆ Books
- ◆ _____
- ◆ _____

Miscellaneous:
- ◆ Toilet paper
- ◆ Tissues
- ◆ Bathroom cleansers
- ◆ _____
- ◆ _____

APPLYING THE MAGIC FORMULA

Now that you've organized your closet and kitchen in the previous two chapters, you're a pro. Do you see a pattern emerging in all of our work together? We're always *eliminating* what we don't need. We are always keeping our possessions in *categories*. And the solutions to keep it all *organized* are related. Master your closet and you can do anything! Why? Because once you understand the Magic Formula (eliminate, categorize, organize), you can apply it to any organizing challenge. In fact, in my classes I tell my students that they would be hard pressed to present an organizing challenge that did not yield to this formula. Are you ready to tackle the bathroom?

STEP ONE: SET THE WORK STAGE

If you have a large bathroom, you may want to spread things out on the floor. If you have a small bathroom, try to use either the countertop or, if possible, set up a small table just outside the bathroom. This is going to take some time, so set aside at least five hours. It would be a disaster if you began at 2 P.M. and had to stop at 3 P.M. when the kids came home from school. Remember, people frequently set themselves up for failure by not taking into account all the facets of a job well done.

STEP TWO: TACKLE ONE CATEGORY AT A TIME

Remember when we did your closet in Chapter 4 and I asked you not to place all of your clothes on the bed? If you haul everything out from under the sink and on the counters, you're going to be emotionally overwhelmed. Begin with a single category from the earlier bathroom list, such as cleansing products.

STEP THREE: ELIMINATE THE EXCESS

When you see all your shampoos in one spot, do you realize that you tend to experiment but stay faithful to one product? Please be ruthless and cast away the excess. If you have several jars of the same item, consolidate them into one. If you have shampoos, soaps, and other unopened products from flights, hotels, gifts, or impulse purchases, give them as gifts or start a box to donate them to a local shelter.

WHEN IN DOUBT, TOSS IT OUT

Body lotions, aftershave, hair conditioners, fragrances, liquid makeup, and other personal products don't have an unlimited shelf life. If something smells bad or has separated, throw it away!

STEP FOUR: ORGANIZE YOUR STUFF

Here is where we have our fun. Do you remember the small plastic containers I suggested you find for your pantry in Chapter 5? They will work wonders here! For example, keep all of your hair styling products in one container. When you are ready to style your hair, you won't have to rummage through every bathroom product you own. It will be a matter of picking up one container and returning it to its designated spot. Depending on the depth of your drawers and the number of your cabinets, this placement will vary.

If your partner has hair products of his own, he can implement the same solution. You'll each want to have different sides of the cabinet area for your own things. In fact, you can each have a different color container for your various products. White and black are the most common colors in stock. There are prettier colors from time to time, but should you need additional containers in the future, the buyer at your store may no longer be stocking a color like purple!

Remember the shelf creator we used in the pantry? It can also be employed here. It's a great way to sort products you both use or, if space permits and products demand, you can each have one.

What about the smaller items you may need? Bobby pins, for example, will get lost tossed in a container. And you want to keep your toothbrush pristine and not have it knocking about with other items. What to do? Remember the handy drawer organizers we used in the kitchen? Voilà—you can line a drawer and create categories with a variety of small containers.

A shelf creator comes in handy in the bathroom, too.

And by now, your label maker will provide a finishing touch to your efforts.

STEP FIVE: MAKING IT ALL FIT

Once you have everything in some kind of container or have at least given it a place to exist in the bathroom (for example, you won't be putting toilet paper in a crate but you will want to designate a set spot for it), you will have to put it all together like a big jigsaw puzzle. Here's a handy rule of thumb: Keep what you use daily in the front of the cabinets. For example, every day you have to deal with your hair so those products need to be in the foreground. Your aromatherapy oils and candles will most likely be brought out on weekends or special occasions. They can live in the back of the cabinets. You don't want to be moving and shuffling multiple containers in the morning. This expenditure of time will defeat our purpose.

SPECIAL CHALLENGES

Every client I work with has a unique collection of some item. I know one gentleman who cuts the stamps off return address envelopes. Another client, a famous actress, has almost 100 tubes of lipstick. Do you catch my drift here? The bathroom is perhaps the most common place to keep a large collection of sometimes experimental body or hair care products. Once you whittle down the collection, you'll need to get it organized.

Let's look at a few examples:

◆ **Gobs of makeup.** I had a friend who always used the word *gobs* to identify anything in multiples. It's a great word to describe the voluminous makeup collections some women have. Please keep what you use on a day-to-day basis at hand. Over the years most women collect makeup bags. Why not keep one put away with evening makeup and perhaps one other with the treasures you just know you will one day come back into fashion? You can store these on a shelf in your closet. And if you don't touch them in a year, toss them. (If you have unused sample-size products such as soaps and shampoos, or other products you haven't opened, consider donating them to a shelter.)

◆ **Under-the-sink clutter.** Make your plumber proud by keeping things here tidy and controlled in containers. All sinks spring leaks from time to time and it is disconcerting, to say the least, to have a stranger hauling our personal possessions out and scattering them across the floor. If you want to store cleansers here, try putting them on a cleaning products caddy. This product is sold in the kitchen or bathroom departments of your local home store. And if toddlers are in the home, be sure this door has a sturdy baby lock.

SPACE SAVER

When you bring products home from the store, discard the outer wrapping. You will be amazed at the amount of space you acquire when you organize your bathroom just by discarding packaging!

◆ **Inadequate laundry hampers.** You'll need a hamper in the master suite, if there's room. The bathroom is an ideal place, as is the master closet. Make sure the hamper is large enough to suit your needs; a small hamper might look pretty, but if it's always overflowing with dirty laundry it won't do the job. If you choose a wicker hamper, be sure to purchase the kind with a removable liner. Not only does it protect your clothes, it gives you a way to transport them to the laundry room. Some two-story homes have chutes that send the dirty items directly to the laundry room. If you are designing or remodeling, see if your contractor can add this handy feature.

◆ **Limited storage space.** Your local home store will have a large selection of items designed to add storage to your bathroom. You might want to shop online, in magazines, newspapers, or in catalogs first to get an idea of what's available. One of my favorite solutions is the shelving unit that fits over the toilet. It can be a great place to store extra towels in a small bathroom. Do you remember the rolling cart used to create a dresser in the closet? If funds are limited and it isn't time to make any expensive purchases for the bathroom that same cart can be used in the bathroom for storage.

◆ **No place to hang up bathrobes and such.** Two good-quality hooks on the back of your bathroom door will enable each of you to have your favorite bathrobes close at hand. If you don't want to attach a hook, there are over-the-door models that will hold two robes and perhaps even a nightgown quite easily. If you are renting, this might be a safer bet.

◆ **Reading matter is everywhere.** If you like to read in the bathroom, keep a small caddy by the toilet to house just a few magazines and perhaps your current book. Don't forget to clean this out monthly. It can easily become a permanent storehouse for back issues!

◆ **Unsightly garbage cans.** No matter what style you choose for your bathroom, be sure the size is adequate to the task. And if possible, keep the container lined. So many lotions and potions are used in the bathroom, they can make the garbage can sticky. In addition, used tissues can be a breeding ground for germs.

◆ **Medications jumble.** When I listed this as a category you might have noted that I separated it out into distinct areas: first aid, cold remedies, prescription medicines, and so on. It's wonderful to keep your first aid supplies handy. You don't want to have to dig through product debris on your way to an aspirin or a Band-Aid. It's equally pointless, however, to have cold remedies at your fingertips all year long. If your linen closet is nearby and the bathroom is small, why not store them there in a nice container?

Prescription drugs are a different story, as they may pose a risk to other family members. If small children are in the home, these medications should be stored up out of their reach and preferably under lock and key. Without this risk, you might want to keep current prescriptions in the medicine cabinet (hence its name).

◆ **Too many people using one bathroom.** Bathrooms that are used by several members of the household pose special problems. To avoid overcrowding the shelves and cabinets with everyone's supplies, consider keeping only essentials such as bathroom cleansers, soap, tissues, and toilet paper in the bathroom proper. Each family member can then use one of the large plastic containers with handles mentioned throughout this book to bring individual morning necessities such as shampoo, deodorant, makeup, and shaving items to the bathroom. Smaller containers can be used for the evening ritual. It goes without saying that each person should tidy up the bathroom before leaving. I have a client whose husband and sons leave wet towels all over the bathroom and frequently create near-flood conditions. This isn't fair to anyone involved!

If you follow these guidelines, I have no doubt you will feel that more space has magically appeared in your bathroom and it's an easier room to share.

A CHILD'S BATHROOM

If you set up your children with organized bathrooms and closets, they will experience the principles of an orderly life. Moreover, if you model the same behavior, they will understand that Mom and Dad practice what they preach. If your bathroom looks like Hurricane Andrew hit it, don't be surprised if your children balk at cleaning up their own.

Here are some tips to get your children's feet firmly planted on the road to an organized bathroom:

- Provide small children with a step stool so they can reach the sink.

- Hang a net above the shower so you can keep bathtub toys in one section.

- Tiny people have toothbrushes, toothpaste, hair clips, and combs just like adults. Introduce your children to the same drawer organizers and containers that you used in your bathroom! They can use them for different products, as they get older.

- As children grow and need to learn responsibility, emptying out their trash and wiping off the bathroom counter each day are wonderful habits to instill.

THE GUEST BATHROOM

If you are lucky enough to have a guest bath or a powder room, I hope you will have some fun decorating it. If you are a romantic person and you have had to temper your taste to suit your spouse, perhaps the guest bath is where you can allow free rein to your romantic side. Or if your spouse is understanding and consents to reside in a pink pleasure palace, perhaps the guest bath can have a cowboy motif? You catch my drift.

The guest bath is also a place to experiment with products. I have a client whose husband is highly allergic to any type of scented product. She can't even wear any cologne. Because she loves all these products, her guests are pampered. The guest bath has scented candles, special soaps, and lotions. There's an extra hairdryer and comb. The shower has a selection of shampoos and conditioners. Because you want to feel nurtured in your home, you'll want to extend the same welcome to those who come to visit.

If you have very little storage in your master bathroom and a large guest bath, why not use the cupboards to store your toilet paper and tissues? In the best of all possible worlds, all paper products would reside in the pantry with other household goods. That way everyone will know where they're stored. This is one solution in the event you don't have a pantry or at the very least one inadequate to the task.

THE LINEN CLOSET

Most times a home is designed with the linen closet residing near the master bath. I prefer to keep sheet sets together. Some of my clients like to put the fitted and flat sheets and one pillowcase inside the second pillowcase. I'm not sold on the visual esthetic of this choice, however in a home with a lot of small children this serves the "god of speed"!

If space allows, keep all the sets for each room on a shelf. This way little Bobby and June don't have to rifle through each other's sets, or yours for that matter, when it comes time to change the bed. Making the bed is, by the way, another wonderful responsibility to give children as soon as they are old enough.

The same shelf dividers that I suggested using in your closet will work perfectly in the linen closet to keep all family members' sheet sets separate. This way if shelves are at a premium more than one family member can occupy the same shelf.

If towels have been purchased for specific bathrooms, it's nice if they can reside in that room. If not, separate shelves and some dividers will keep the towels visually appealing and easy to retrieve from the linen closet. Be sure and keep sets together here as well.

While you're cleaning out this area, be sure to check for frayed towels and worn sheets. Is it time to replenish your stock? Sleeping on old linens cannot possibly make you feel good about yourself, much less nurtured. Towels can always be used for the pets in the home or for rags. Old sheets can be used as floor covering while you repaint a room!

DONATE OLD LINENS

If you have a lot of old towels, blankets, and other linens that have seen better days, consider donating them to an animal shelter. You'll rest easier knowing you've made a dog's or cat's life a little more comfortable.

NOTHING IS SACRED

I had a wonderful client who traveled a lot on business. Inevitably, John would purchase one or two new shirts to add to his collection in the city where he had a meeting. When it came time to organize his closet, I was faced with a problem. The walk-in would accommodate just about all of his possessions except for one category. John had more shirts than most department stores! His hanging shirts would fit into his closet, but the new ones and those returned from the cleaners would have no room.

Right outside his walk-in clothes closet, however, was a huge linen closet—the largest I have ever seen! Thankfully, John and his wife did not have a large selection of linens. The bathrooms were large enough to house their own towels. Just down the hall from the master, we used a smaller linen closet designed for the guest rooms to house all the bed linens for the home. Now I had that huge linen closet with floor-to-ceiling shelves for John's folded shirts! He was delighted. They were arranged in a beautiful, color-coordinated display that was at once visually appealing and functional.

The moral of the story: Remember to think creatively even when you are organizing the lowly linen closet.

AN UNEXPECTED TOUCH

I have a friend whose home is filled with modern art. Some of her pieces are pure whimsy. The most amazing aspect of her collection is its accessibility. You never feel as if you are in an art gallery or a museum. From the moment you enter, you sense that you are in a warm and inviting home.

One night as I was about to exit the guest bathroom, I was amused to see a half-empty container of popcorn sitting on the back of the toilet tank. *More whimsy!* I thought and exited with a big smile on my face. I said to my friend, "Only you would have popcorn in the bathroom. What a funny touch!" "No," said my friend. "It isn't for fun. It's feng shui!"

Have you been sick lately? Do you feel run down? Would you like to replace some of the energy expended while sitting on "the throne"? Popcorn to the rescue! Place a container of unpopped popcorn on the back of your toilet tank. Fill it only three quarters so that there is room for more: an important aspect of the symbolic language at play. Be sure there is a lid. For an extra special touch, tie a red ribbon around the container. Be sure the ribbon is measured in increments of 9; that is, 9 inches or 18 inches, and so on. I'll explain the philosophy in Chapter 11 when we discuss feng shui. For now, feel free to add a touch of whimsy and good luck in your bathroom!

FINAL NOTE

Make it your goal to treat your body with the honor and respect it so richly deserves. Your bathrooms need to be organized on the outside where your towels and everyday products live out in the open. They also need to have the inner world of drawers and cupboards support that outer organization. This is a guiding rule of thumb for the entire house that can be forgotten in this most important of rooms.

7

THE COMMON ROOMS

"When we truly care for ourselves, it becomes possible to care far more profoundly about other people. The more alert and sensitive we are to our own needs, the more loving and generous we can be toward others."

—Eda LeShan, American writer

Ideally, the common rooms in your home—such as the living room, family room, den, or finished basement—are where you relax with your family and entertain your friends. Here is where we're likely to find stereo systems, DVD players, TVs, and other recreational toys. Someone in the home may display a hobby or have a book collection in this room.

Keeping these common rooms organized should be a simple matter of picking up a few tips and tricks, don't you think? Sadly, though, these rooms frequently turn into war zones. Is it that way in your house?

COMMON SENSE

If the common rooms in your home are in need of a makeover, please start by answering the following questions in your journal to see if you can get a better handle on your situation.

1. Do you currently spend any significant time in the living room?

2. Is the living room used exclusively for formal occasions like holidays?

3. Would you like to make the living room more accessible for family and friends?

4. Is your family room constantly in an uproar?

5. Could you eliminate some furniture in the family room?

6. Do you actually need some extra pieces in the family room to increase your storage capacity?

7. Do you have too many possessions in the family room for it to be inviting?

8. Does everyone in the family pitch in to keep the family room tidy?

9. Is your den serving a special purpose (for example, as a home office, gym, sewing room, or crafts room)?

10. Does the den serve so many special purposes that no one can use it as a place to relax?

11. Did you finish your basement only to have it turn into a storage room?

12. If you do want to use the basement for storage, did you set it up with adequate shelving and tables?

Let's examine each of these areas and the traditional ways they are used. Please read each section, because the information might be applicable to you in a different area of your home. You might not have all of these rooms, but you might have most of these possessions and challenges.

THE FORMAL LIVING ROOM

When I was growing up, a formal living room was a given. My mother had exquisite taste and our living room was especially lovely to behold. It was a shame that during the course of the year, you could count on both hands the number of times anyone used that room. We always said it was a pity. We just never did anything about it! Many of the larger homes I see today have a scaled-down version of the formal living room. The room tends to be small in size and is decorated in that "please do not touch" way that immediately eliminates all children and pets.

If you do a lot of formal entertaining, you will need this room almost as an adjunct to your business life. Here is where you will keep your bar, liquor, and glassware for after-dinner drinks. If you have a large book collection, this is a great place to keep your coffee table and special collection books on display. Many of my clients have unique hobbies or collections that lend a special grace to the room. I can call to mind a female client with an exquisite collection of Japanese netsukes, the tiny Asian hand carved sculptures that are delicate and detailed. Another male client was truly one of the last of the "great white hunters" and his living room boasted various types of African animal heads. As you can see, this is a wide-open category. The bottom line is that you get to choose what you will reveal about yourself to others.

EASY CLEANING

Try to use stain-resistant fabrics and carpeting in the living room. If there is an accident such as a dropped glass of wine, it doesn't have to be a disaster.

Plants will always add a touch of warmth to any room. In the case of a rarely used room like this, at least you'll be walking in once or twice a week to water them! In Chapter 11, I'll tell you about feng shui, the Chinese art of placement. You'll see how it's best to keep the energy in all the rooms of your home active and strong. A room that is left like an orphan will have a lonely, disconnected feeling to it. In feng shui this is called stagnant energy. Why not come up with an activity that you can start performing in your formal living room? Here is a list of things that are basically mess-free that you might now be doing in other rooms:

- ◆ Needlepointing
- ◆ Crocheting
- ◆ Knitting
- ◆ Writing letters, thank you notes, or invitations
- ◆ Reading
- ◆ Meditating

Consider the possibility. You might discover a secret haven right in your own home!

THE FAMILY ROOM

Today's homes are being designed with larger and larger family rooms. In fact, many now open right into the kitchen, a design I personally embrace. In still other modern designs, the family room has replaced the formal living room. Everyone comes here to relax after a good meal! Let's assume you have both. What can we do to solve the common problems this room usually harbors? See if the following suggestions can help you create a more peace-filled environment for family and friends.

CHILDREN'S TOYS

Many parents encourage their children to play in the family room. If you are one of them, please supply storage space for the games, stuffed animals, and other items that will now inhabit this area. Otherwise, you will be faced with a constant cyclone and casual drop-bys will cause panic in your psyche.

One of the handiest ways to sort toys for small children (automatically teaching them, by the way, about categories) is to use inexpensive large crates or, my personal favorite, heavy plastic containers with lids. Be careful not to stack any type of container if the children are very young. You don't want them to reach for a toy and be knocked out by a cascade of toys and containers. If you and your partner each bring small children into the union, why not get containers in different colors so that each child can have a clear, personal area in which to store his or her things? Teach children to sort toys by type: stuffed animals, Legos, Barbies, blocks, etc.

These sturdy storage cubes are great for organizing toys.

ENLISTING CHILDREN'S HELP

One day my best friend and I were working on the setup of the original manuscript for my first book, *The Zen of Organizing*. Because I am a computer moron, Susie asked me to play with her then two-year-old daughter Molly while she noodled on the computer with the presentation of the material. In a few hours, Molly and I were called to dinner. Imagine my surprise when pint-size

Molly announced to me that before we could leave her room she had to pick up her toys.

Molly was too young to notice that her Auntie Regina was stunned. I watched as she quietly put books back on her bookcase, toys into crates, and stuffed animals back into her crib. When I asked her mother how in the world she had trained her two-year-old to do that, she proudly told me that even at day care the children were asked to be responsible for cleaning up after play. Molly had been getting the message for more than a year from all the adults in her life.

If you have trouble getting your children to pick up after themselves, I have some questions for you to answer in your journal. I hear this complaint from parents more than any other: "How can I get my kids to pick up/help around the house? They refuse." Are you ready? This can be a challenging yet rewarding subject.

1. Do you allow your children to choose whether they should help? Do you think it should be their choice?

2. Are there rewards for helping and consequences for refusing your requests? Do you enforce these consequences? Do these rewards and consequences matter to your children? Are they impactful? Is it time to adjust rewards and consequences, or create new ones?

3. Have you ever contemplated how your children will be able to take care of themselves and their environments when they leave home? I'm sure you don't plan on doing their laundry until they find a willing spouse.

4. Are you avoiding something in your life by doing all the household work, not letting anyone else participate?

5. Are you a perfectionist and do you find it difficult to let your children help?

6. Did your mother mirror this pattern of behavior in your childhood home?

7. If your response to #6 was "yes," how did you feel watching your mother do all the work?

8. If your response to #6 was "no," what prompted you to alter the parental behavior you saw as a child? We all make a choice to either emulate our parents or rebel against them.

After the untimely death of John F. Kennedy Jr., one of his former college housemates, correspondent Christine Ammampour, was telling an anecdote about him on *60 Minutes*. I almost fell off my couch when she said they all took turns doing housework. Even John F. Kennedy Jr. had a turn at cleaning toilets. It puts it all into perspective, doesn't it?

If this is a sensitive area for you, I have no doubt that a host of related issues might surface as you do this work. Please feel free to continue your journal work on your own. If you are seeing a therapist, these entries might prompt a conversation during your next session. You might also want to have your spouse answer these questions. If not in a journal (not everyone will be comfortable with the format), perhaps during a discussion, you can ask these questions and make your discoveries.

A UNITED FRONT

Rearing children takes tremendous energy. You and your partner should agree on a plan of action when it comes to rules, regulations, and expectations for the home and its inhabitants.

FAMILY-FRIENDLY FURNITURE

You'll want to invest in more casual furniture for the family room. Priceless antiques and designer sofas will put a crimp in your ability to kick back and relax with some popcorn during a movie! It's also helpful if the furniture can serve multiple purposes. Here are some suggestions for furnishing the family room:

◆ Purchase a sofa that opens up to accommodate sleepover guests. Be sure the fabric is treated with stain protector.

◆ Get a coffee table with drawers and use them to store some of your entertainment collections (CDs, videos, etc.) or children's toys.

◆ Try to secure an entertainment unit for the TV. This will enable you to close the TV behind doors when not in use. These units frequently come with shelf space and drawers, offering more help for those entertainment collections.

◆ Encourage your children to read by keeping a bookcase in this room. If space and finances allow, perhaps bookcases can be built into an entire wall.

◆ Remember that bookcases can house popular entertainment collections as well as books. You might want to purchase some small containers to place on the shelves. Another idea is to have a bookcase on one wall and simple shelves over closed cabinets on another. You can play with this arrangement. For example, you might have a bookcase on either side of closed cabinets on one long wall. The shelves over the cabinets might be used to display decorative items while the bookcase shelves are strictly utilitarian.

◆ Be sure your carpet is stain resistant. You don't want to have to make a federal case out of every spill and mess.

◆ Place a chest behind the couch. This is a clever place to store board games and other items.

◆ Whether you are designing any of the previously mentioned pieces or searching for them in the store, try to find units with adjustable shelves so you can house VHS tapes, books, and other different-size items.

◆ Be sure you don't have too many pieces of furniture in the family room. Perhaps you need to eliminate some furniture to create a little floor space. Instead of the look of a furniture store, you can add an area for dancing to the room!

◆ Ask yourself if you have too many pieces of furniture to handle a single task. Instead of multiple small CD holders, for example, try one large bookcase for your CD collection.

◆ Purchase or use existing furniture that can take a beating from your children. They need a place where they need to be respectful and yet a little less careful than, say, in your formal dining room.

PHOTOS AND MEMORABILIA

Why not create an area in your family room where you work on photo albums? You won't need much more than a good size desk and a comfortable chair. Remember that unit on wheels we used in the closet to create a makeshift dresser (see Chapter 4)? Why not keep one by your desk to store scrapbook accessories? Most craft stores carry acid-free photo albums and supplies that will ensure that your photos and mementos will last a lifetime.

It's really nice to work your sentimental treasures into your albums to create a kind of scrapbook. For example, let's say you take the train from Paris to the south of France and you insist on saving those ticket stubs (you know who you are!). Instead of tucking your train stubs into a box marked "Trip to France," why not put the receipts next to the photos you place in the album? It really makes an album come alive when the pages are broken up with sentimental keepsakes. Here's another example: Your Aunt Tilly passes away and you create a special section in an album in honor of her. Did she ever send you a note? Why not attach it to a page in this section? When friends see the photos of famous Aunt Tilly, they are going to feel as if they knew her.

By the way, as you complete your albums, you can use some of the shelf space we talked about earlier to store them. Instead of being tucked away for posterity, your family and friends can actually enjoy your albums.

Speaking of being tucked away, it really is more than under-standable to save some things that are personal and private to you. I have, for example, all the letters my father wrote to me after he retired. I have no idea what prompted me to save them. They are safely put away in a box of special treasures. Every few years I take them out and read them. They mean more to me than I have words to express. Being sentimental, however, does not mean you should give yourself license to save everything. If I had every piece of paper my dad ever wrote on, every article of clothing he ever wore, and every possession he ever owned, I would still not have my father back. Be selective in the way you remember your departed loved ones. Give some thought to how you wish to be remembered. Share those desires with your family. Don't let your legacy be truckloads of stuff you never took the time to deal with.

MUSIC COLLECTIONS

The easiest way to store records, cassette tapes, CDs, etc., is alpha-betically by artist. However, if your collection is extensive, this might be more order than you can deal with, so try these variations:

♦ Divide your music collections into categories and then keep your categories together. For example, Female Country Western Singers is a category and Male Hip Hop Artists would be another.

♦ Designate physical areas in your home for various types of music. Do the kids congregate in the family room with their friends? This is the perfect place for the music that defines their generation. Perhaps your bedroom is the place for your Beatles collection? Maybe you'll want that mood music in your home office? See how creative you can be with your collection.

♦ If you and your partner came into the relationship with a lot of duplicates, you have the luxury of having that Beatles col-lection in your family room *and* the bedroom. Don't keep them together. It will take up too much space. Or consider donating duplicates to a charity or selling them online.

◆ If you no longer have a record player but want to keep your vinyl record collection, store it out of the busy family areas where space is surely at a premium. You can purchase special boxes made for this purpose. Do not stack your collection or store it in an area of the home that is subject to dampness or humidity, such as an unfinished basement or the garage. Vinyl can easily be affected by the elements and pressure.

DVDS, VHS TAPES, AND VIDEO GAMES

Storing these in alphabetical order works well, too, although you may have trouble getting everyone in the family to cooperate. You might, once again, wish to create categories and simply keep related products together. Here the categories would be something along the lines of drama, comedy, action-adventure, documentary, soaps, and games. Just as with your music collection, you might find that certain tapes or DVDs are of interest to isolated members of the family. Mom might want to get caught up on her soaps in the privacy of the master bedroom while Junior wants to watch the latest action movie in his room. You can figure this out while you are sorting the entire collection. The guidelines for duplicates are the same as for music.

Do you have a stash of unlabeled mystery tapes? Box them up for a rainy day when you will have time to go through them. I actually gave mine the heave-ho a few years ago. Each tape had six hours of material. In what universe would I be able to spend that kind of time looking at old programs? The only caveat here is that you must be sure that no family functions are in the group you are considering for the trash. You wouldn't want to offer to show the video of your wedding and suddenly realize it was mistakenly given the heave-ho in an organizing frenzy!

You can always prop a few tapes near the TV in case someone needs to tape a program. Now that you have your handy label maker, the contents will never be a mystery again! If the program you copy is one you know you won't be holding on to, I would use a less permanent way to keep track of the contents of the tape. You might, for instance, write the contents on a Post-it and place it in the VHS sleeve with the tape.

HOBBIES/COLLECTIONS

It's wonderful to share a private part of yourself with your family and friends. Just be sure you don't overwhelm the room with your things. Remember that the goal here is a room that reflects the family, not the most powerful person in it. Let the wall space, the shelves, and the storage areas reflect all the members of the household.

I have two clients with overpowering personal collections. One elderly gentleman had truly been one of the last great white hunters in Africa. Animal heads were mounted on every available wall space in his home. His wife was less than thrilled. Another client had an extensive collection of expensive and elegant Madame Alexander dolls. Her husband couldn't escape them; like a fungus, they exploded all over the house. In each of these scenarios, a personal passion has infringed on the space of the other partner.

THE DEN

In today's world, the den generally suffers an identity crisis. In the days before an official family room was included in the design of the home, this was the casual "kick back and relax" room. Today, many consider making the den a home office. They put an inadequate desk and an empty file cabinet in the room, which sit idle waiting to be used. Maybe you considered making the den into a gym? Sadly, after the equipment arrived, I would bet that no one really used it. Has something like this happened in your den?

The first order of business is to decide how you want the room to function. If your den is the family room, then the instructions in the previous sections will assist you in setting it up. If you'd like to use it as an office and a gym (this is the most popular combination), is there adequate space for both? Whatever activity you wish to perform in this room you will need to plan.

Basically, you need to understand what you need to perform the desired activity well. You'll want to measure the room and see if, after placing the listed items, you have any room left for a second activity. And finally, you might discover that some of the items in the room must be removed. Let's see what this looks like. I am going to use the office and gym example because they are such a popular combination. You might have a craft and sewing room instead. The guidelines are the same.

Office Requirements	**Home Gym Requirements**
Adequate desk	Treadmill
Comfortable chair	Weight bench
Computer or laptop	Large mirror
Good lighting	Free weights and stand
File cabinet	TV and VCR/DVD player
Area rug	
Bookcase	
Office supplies	

Items That Need to Be Removed

Old sofa

Old coffee table

Worn-out easy chair

Camping equipment (no longer used)

Ski equipment (used once)

Now that you have a plan, decide what you need to make it a reality. In our hypothetical example, there is a lot of furniture and miscellaneous equipment that a charity would appreciate. You could make arrangements for them to pick up the furniture.

Perhaps a neighborhood teen would like to take up skiing or go camping? Make that your second phone call.

Make a rough sketch of the room and see how you can most advantageously set it up to accommodate its new purpose. What do you need to purchase? What do you already have? If you have everything you need, get some help (perhaps that grateful teenager has a burly friend?) and start setting up the room. If you need to go shopping, schedule that time in your calendar or day planner and watch the newspapers for sales.

CRAFT A WINNING PLAN

Beyond making your den into a room you can truly enjoy, you can learn how to make your dreams come true by creating step-by-step plans that turn them into reality. This is good practice. You can do this with any room or aspect of your life.

THE FINISHED BASEMENT

When I was growing up in Brooklyn, it was quite the thing when someone announced they had a finished basement. The upstairs was the mother's showplace for company. The family and close friends played and relaxed downstairs in the finished basement. This was another forerunner of today's family room. If you have a finished basement, you may have part of it for family use and the rest looks like a storage facility. Am I close?

The downside to this arrangement is that the room looks and feels chaotic. It just isn't fun to be there, is it? In addition, all the decisions you refused to make about furniture, clothing, and toys get dumped in the basement. In feng shui it's said that the entire home is affected by the indecision that rises from the foundation of the home. Take a minute to think about your family dynamic. Is there a lot of indecision in your home life? Is there a charity or friend who could benefit from the items you have stored here?

THE WISE WAITRESS

Let me digress for a moment to tell you about a young woman I met a few years ago. She said, "I would never date a man who wasn't a generous tipper." I laughed, assuming this reflected her years as a waitress rather than a serious statement about perspective mates. I asked why she felt that way. She then said something I never forgot. Indeed it's become a part of my philosophy: "The way a person does one thing is the way he does everything."

If everything we do is part of the total picture of our personality, isn't every chaotic corner of our homes a reflection of an inner chaos? We may be clever and hide it from the world by keeping it hidden in the basement, but that doesn't mean it no longer exists. I hope this gives you extra incentive to restore order to a room you may not physically enter or use very often. I am going to bet you will as soon as it is divested of old, unwanted, outworn possessions.

THE HALL CLOSET

I have included the hall closet in this chapter because it is an area shared by family and friends. Here are some tips for keeping this area in order:

◆ Keep your coats on uniform hangers. Wooden ones work best for coats and jackets.

◆ Have a shoe rack in the closet to prevent an explosion of shoes on the floor.

◆ Tuck a small (albeit tall) wastebasket in the corner if you have a large family with many umbrellas. Keep them here. Toss the top of the can.

◆ Don't forget to add a second shelf for storage. We have discussed any number of items for safekeeping here. Be creative!

◆ On the lower shelf, keep small harvest baskets with liners or plastic containers for gloves, hats, and scarves. On cold winter mornings, getting out of the house with an entire cold weather wardrobe will be easier.

◆ If space permits, attach some hooks to the wall. Baseball caps, pet leashes, and the like can hang here.

◆ Group your coats: Hang the jackets together, then raincoats, and finally long winter coats. If you have a lot of coats, you can further group them according to color, if you like.

FINAL NOTE

It might take more communication between you and your partner to set up the shared or common areas of the home than it will to establish the private areas. In general, men aren't very concerned about the bedroom or the bathrooms. Most men rarely cook or do so only on weekends or holidays. These rooms are usually the provinces of the woman in the home. In the common areas, however, we really mix up our stuff, don't we? The watchword is *respect*. It isn't your family room, or his den, or the kids' basement. These are the common parts of your home. With the idea of sharing your good fortune with family and friends as your goal, I have no doubt you will be successful.

8

THE CHILDREN'S ROOMS AND GUEST ROOM

"To live life ... with dignity, to celebrate and accept responsibility for your presence in the world is all that can be asked of anyone."

—*August Wilson, American playwright and poet*

I am a baby boomer. My generation was raised with scholastic expectations, household chores, and consequences when we did not do as we were told. When I talk to other boomers, we all agree there were two basic reasons we did as we were told: those famous consequences and respect for our parents. I saw my father go to work every day, and I heard him tell my mother about his job when he returned home. I understood that he wasn't at a picnic. He worked hard to provide for us. I never wanted to see disappointment in his eyes—or my mother's for that matter.

I watched my mother pour herself into her home. I remember she always complained about having to wash lingerie every night by hand. As a child the solution seemed to me to be simple: Don't do it! When I asked my mother why she did things she didn't enjoy, her answer was always the same: "They need to be done and I don't have a fairy godmother. Who will do it if I don't?" Today, as an adult I frequently think of my mother's words and laugh to myself as I do chores I would really rather avoid. The fairy godmother seems to have lost my address as well!

THE REAL WORLD

As a writer I was hired to produce this book. I was given a deadline for submitting not only the manuscript but also the illustrations. I scheduled my time and came through for my publisher. The consequence for getting behind would have been twofold: many people in the creative pipeline would, in turn, get behind in their scheduled contributions to the book and we would not make the publication target date. In addition, I would not have been paid. My creditors are not interested in my good intentions. They need payment every month.

Where did I learn how to plan and schedule? Who taught me about responsibility and consequences? My parents were the principal architects of this philosophy that is so ingrained in my nature. It is your responsibility to teach your children.

Parents who wail, "I *ask* my child to do something but he refuses!" are missing the boat. How will this child become a productive member of society? How will he turn in school assignments on time? What will happen when he has assignments at his place of employment? Perhaps most basic of all is the issue of household chores. If you never learn how to make a bed, wash a dish, vacuum, sweep, take out the garbage, or do laundry, what kind of living quarters will you create as an adult? Household chores are a microcosm of all the tasks one must perform in the course of a lifetime. Home is your training ground.

It is equally true that chores build self-esteem. One day you toddle around putting your toys into containers. Before long, you are making your bed and soon you can do your own laundry. Children long to be treated like adults. What better way can you think to have them earn the privileges of adult life? Being an adult isn't a chronological consideration; it is rather an ability to be self-sufficient in the world.

Now a word of caution: If you plan on scheduling a "family summit" in order to lay down the law and you yourself are not organized, don't take another step in this direction. As an example, if you ask your child to make his bed and empty the garbage can in his bedroom on a daily basis and you don't do that in your bedroom, guess what? He probably won't bother. It is obviously not important to you. Teaching by example is the most powerful method I know of influencing children. This is why guidelines for children's rooms are toward the back of both of my books. You need to take care of yourself first before you can teach someone else.

PARABLE OF THE BABY CHICKS

This story was told to me many years ago. I have no idea whether it is true or apocryphal. In any event, the message is very powerful. I hope you will take it to heart.

A chicken farmer was incubating eggs. A terrible thing began to happen that caused him to go to his local vet in a panic. "My baby chicks are too weak to mature normally," cried the farmer. "I have no idea what is wrong. Can you help me?" The vet agreed to come to the farm and see the chicks for himself.

Upon his arrival, he was amazed to find the perfect setup. The incubator was large and the temperature was correct. He began to ask the farmer some questions to see if he could get to the root of the problem. "Are you doing anything to the eggs?" asked the vet. "Well," said the farmer proudly, "when I see the first cracks in the shell, I help them along. I break open the shell for the chicks." The vet smiled wearily. "As baby chicks break open the egg, they strengthen their beaks. This enables them to eat normally once they are hatched. Your intentions were good, but your actions have crippled the chicks."

Be careful not to let your love for your children cripple their ability to care for themselves in the world.

CHILDREN'S CHORES

Throughout this book I have casually tossed out things that would be great chores for the children in the house. Let's take a look at a list of suggestions. You can add or subtract items depending on the size of your home. A toddler can put away his toys. A teenager with a driver's license can help grocery shop. Match the chore to the age of the children in your home.

Household Chores

Pick up toys and put them away

Wash dishes

Dry dishes

Put dishes away

Empty dishwasher

Dust

Vacuum

Sweep

Take out garbage

Make bed

Tidy bedroom

Tidy family room

Do laundry

Fold laundry

Grocery shop

Put groceries away

Cook (some or full preparation, depending on age)

Set the table for meals

Clear the table after a meal

Feed and care for the family pet(s)

Water indoor plants

Yard Chores

Water lawn and plants

Rake leaves

Mow the lawn

Weed flowerbeds and gardens

Fill bird feeders

Shovel snow

Wash family car

Clean porch furniture

THE PRIVATE WORLD OF A CHILD

I am a huge proponent of a child having his own room. I also believe he should have some autonomy in that space as he grows older. I don't mean that it's okay if the bed is never made, clothes are draped over the furniture, or food rots under the bed! I do mean he should be able to have a say in the furniture he lives with and the decorations on the walls. It is in this space that we begin to separate from the styles that attracted our parents. We all need a sanctuary within the home.

Let's look at the elements in the typical child's room.

FURNITURE

It isn't necessary to purchase overly expensive or antique furniture for a small child or even a teenager. Children have to learn respect for possessions. They also need coordination! Things take time. Why not let them relax in a world that doesn't belong in *Architectural Digest?*

I have a client whose son has remarkable artistic talent. When they moved into their new house, she said he could do some artwork on the walls if he brought her a plan. He wrote a story and created characters that he drew in a border in his room. Your child might not have this kind of talent, but he might wish to express himself in other ways in his private world. Perhaps he would like special linens for the bed that have his favorite cartoon characters on them, or she would enjoy a bookshelf to showcase her special treasures. Just as you walk into your home at night and feel comforted by the things that express who you are, your child needs to discover himself and feel comforted in his private world.

TEAMWORK

Does your child love arts and crafts? Why not purchase an unfinished dresser and sponge paint it together? Or perhaps you have a budding sports start in your household. Why not put up a basketball net and schedule some pick-up games after dinner, or invite some kids over for a little touch football on the weekend?

CLOSET ORGANIZATION

The guidelines for organizing your closet will work well here. Please make certain adjustments for small children. For example, their clothes are so small, you will best be served by having double hanging capacity rather than a space for long clothing. Young children will want to help themselves, so be sure you have a sturdy step stool in the closet. In fact, you'll need one in the child's bathroom as well.

Purchase one color and type of hanger for your child's clothing so that the look in his closet is as restful as that in your closet. For small children, smaller-size hangers are available that can better accommodate their petite clothes. You might want to store clothing in your child's dresser and use a portable unit on wheels in his closet for small items that he'll need every day like socks and underwear. As your children grow, they will exert more and more influence over what they wear. In the beginning, while you are making the decisions, at least they can get the everyday items for themselves.

TOY STORAGE

The guidelines in the previous chapter on toys will apply here as well. Some parents prefer that their children play in their rooms rather than any other location in the home. Other parents want the child's room to be a quiet zone and have all the toys in the family room. There is no right or wrong. What is crucial is that a place exists for every toy and game. Once a child is old enough to take his toys out, he is old enough to put them away.

Here are some tips for storing toys:

◆ Free up floor space by hanging a mesh hammock in the bathroom and/or bedroom to store bath toys, soft toys, and stuffed animals.

◆ Remember that a bookcase can hold board games as well as books. Keep them on the bottom shelves.

◆ Keep the board games the family uses in the common areas and let your child keep a few others in his room. As he grows older, he might want to have friends over and share certain games with them.

◆ If you have blended families and duplicate toys, you might want to give some to a charity and help a family in need. You might have siblings or friends with children who can "recycle" the toys into their homes. Or you can have a popular board game in the common room *and* in a child's room.

◆ Heavy-duty plastic bins with wheels are wonderful for children's toys, especially those multi-piece wonders like Legos. Teach your child to respect her things. Today it's respect for a plastic toy container; tomorrow it's respect for a laptop!

- Consider having your child give one toy away every time he receives a new one for his birthday or during the holiday season in December. This act not only teaches generosity, it fosters an appreciation for a personal environment that isn't cluttered with possessions.

- Purchase a toy chest carefully: You don't want the lid to be too heavy or have a hinge that automatically snaps the lid shut. It might be too heavy and pinch tiny fingers.

SHARING A ROOM

The watchword here is *respect*. Children sharing a room are going to have to divide the space into zones. You might want to use area rugs here as we did elsewhere in the home to divide the space visually. They will need the freedom to express themselves in their personal space. Children should be equally responsible for keeping the area tidy.

Siblings squabble. No professional organizer can devise a physical plan for a room that will eliminate that aspect of growing up. We can, however, organize the possessions in that room so that they follow the guidelines for every area of the home. The area should be beautiful to look at so that you feel mentally calm and refreshed just being in the space. We want everything organized so that what you need is at your fingertips. And we want it to be a snap to maintain as possessions shift with time. Toys, clothing, or kitchen pots and pans—it's all the same!

OFF TO A SUCCESSFUL START

Today a child shares a room with a sibling. Tomorrow she goes off to college and shares a dorm room. One day she's working in corporate America and shares an office. As a parent, you lay the groundwork for her ability to successfully cope in all these arenas. And it starts in her personal space.

RUNNING A TIGHT SHIP

My friend Tanya the chef was one of eight children growing up in Chicago. Her mother ran a tight ship. At night each child had a task to perform at dinnertime. One set the table, another helped cook, another helped serve the meal, while another took out the trash and so on. Not only was everyone involved, the chores rotated on a weekly basis.

Household responsibilities were not confined to kitchen chores. Each child had to clean the room he shared with a sibling. He was also responsible for keeping his hidden world organized. What do I mean by "hidden world"? This would be the closet and the drawers in the room. Actually any area hidden from the view of the casual visitor qualifies. Tanya says her mother did spot checks of their drawers. She would come home from school and find the contents of a drawer on her bed. Her mother never said a word. The unspoken message was clear. Less really is more, don't you think? No nagging, no arguments, no pleading—just the sight of an upturned drawer.

My friend Lynn's mothering skills are nothing shy of awesome. She was divorced when her third child was only a few months old. She, too, ran a tight ship. For many years all three children shared a room. There was never any question which area of the room was used by which child. The sections were as distinct as the children themselves. One day I asked Lynn how she managed to be so strict. It takes energy, focus, and commitment on the part of a parent. I admired her. She looked at me incredulously and said, "One day I will have three teenagers in this house. If I don't have control now, I'll be lost later." Words to live by.

I hope these stories have inspired you. By the way, these mothers and others I have known had a wonderful system of rewards and consequences in place. Stuck for ideas? I'll get you started and you add your preferences. I don't think that money or candy is a great reward for a child. An allowance commensurate with the child's age and personal needs should be given but getting paid to perform chores seems inappropriate. Family members need to pitch in for the good of the entire family. If a child wishes to earn some extra money in addition to his allowance, he needs to do something above and beyond his normal chores. Candy is loaded with sugar. It can rot small teeth, get children overly excited, and create a lifelong addiction to sugar. Giving candy as a reward is an easy fix but not necessarily a wise one.

Here are some suggested rewards for a job well done:

◆ Healthy snacks (moderate portions of fresh fruit, nuts, raisins, etc.)

◆ Special meal (getting to pick the menu or restaurant)

◆ Toys, computer games, etc.

◆ Play date with a favorite friend

◆ Outing with a parent (without other kids in the family)

◆ Stickers

◆ Reward points leading to a treat like a day at the zoo, amusement park, or mall

◆ Extra privileges (extra TV or computer time, staying up a few minutes past bedtime on weekends)

◆ Special, extra reading time with parents (child gets to pick his favorite book)

Here are some suggested consequences for *not* doing a job:

◆ Loss of privileges (includes loss of TV, computer, and phone time)

◆ Extra chores added to personal responsibilities for the week or the same chore is repeated for an extended period of time (for example, if a child does not take out the garbage on Thursday, you might give him that chore for another week or add mowing the lawn over the next weekend)

◆ The time-honored consequence: being grounded

◆ Time-out/quiet time

Most parenting magazines can give you additional suggestions about age appropriate rewards and consequences.

CHORE CHARTS

One of my clients has a wonderful way of teaching her children about time and personal commitments. She hangs an extra large calendar on the back of the kitchen door. All three children know where the calendar is located. They also know not to share its existence with their friends. You see social engagements are logged here for each child. Their thoughtful mother has taught them not to hurt the feelings of a visitor by letting them see a party scheduled to which they have not been invited. This is the perfect place to indicate daily chores, especially if there are multiple children in the family and responsibilities rotate.

You can have this calendar in your kitchen or family room. Here is an easy way each child can learn that time is a commodity that must be used wisely. If it is frittered away there is no way to get it back. This calendar is the perfect location to log not only social activities and chores but after-school commitments as well. Everyone in the family will know the whereabouts of the other family members at a glance. In the event of an emergency, you will more easily be able to develop a plan to gather all family members together.

On this same calendar you can attach a paper with critical names and numbers. This list should include not only other family members but also trusted friends and family physicians. If at all possible, please create this document in the computer. It can be run off easily when copies are needed and no one will have to struggle to read your handwriting. As your children get older, they can be responsible for their own schedules in their personal day planners/calendars. Once again a simple solution to a present need evolves into a useful life skill for your child.

PETS: THOSE OTHER MEMBERS OF THE FAMILY

I wanted to say a word about animals in this section because most children ask for a pet. If you are not experienced with animals, please do a little homework before you make an emotional decision about the newest member of your family. With today's expert animal care, dogs, cats, birds, and indeed all domesticated pets can live long, healthy, happy lives. A pet becomes a member of your household. It will require an emotional, physical, and financial commitment on your part for many years to come. The rewards of owning a pet are too numerous to mention—and taking care of a family pet is a wonderful way for your children to learn responsibility. The love they receive in return can't help but make for a better human being.

Let's talk about dogs for a moment, because that is the animal I have the most experience with. Every breed is unique. I am the proud owner of a Golden Retriever named Katie. This breed is smart, loving, loyal, and great with children. A Golden Retriever is in the "field dog" classification. This means my Katie is genetically programmed to hunt for birds and squirrels. Nature tells her to run six feet in front of me and cover the ground, seeking the scent of prey. Field dogs require more exercise than most breeds. Therefore, I walk Katie one to three miles every day. A good rule of thumb for all breeds is: A tired dog is a good dog!

Contact some animal rescue organizations and/or a trainer recommended by a friend. Tell them what you offer a pet and ask them to suggest some breeds that will flourish in this environment. If you cannot take care of your animal's particular needs, select a different one. For example, if I throw a ball around a large backyard, I can wear out a Teacup Poodle in about 15 minutes. You see the difference? Your pet will become a loyal and cherished member of the family. It deserves to be chosen with care.

Here are some questions to consider in your journal before making your selection.

1. What household conditions do you offer a pet? For example, do you have a backyard or do you live in an apartment?

2. Are you home most of the day? How many hours each day will the animal be required to be alone? Dogs are social animals and need lots of love and attention. Even large birds like cockatiels and parrots require human companionship. Again, research your pet choice carefully. The addition of an animal to your home should never be done on impulse.

3. Do you have an adequate budget for food, toys, spaying or neutering, and regular vet care? What about emergencies?

4. Who will take the dog to obedience school? A good dog is a trained dog. Katie frequently came to work with me when she was younger. Everyone would exclaim, "I want a dog just like Katie." Katie and I shared a secret. When I adopted her she was a one-year-old "wild thing." In fact, I felt that was her personal theme song! We spent 20 consecutive weeks in school learning how to communicate with each other. Are you ready to make such a commitment? Dogs are nurtured and trained to reach their potential. Much like children, they do not exit the womb ready for the world.

5. Have you decided if the pet will be allowed on the furniture? Here is an area in which you and your partner might disagree. Work this out before the animal arrives.

6. How does your partner feel about getting a pet? Will he or she pitch in with the care?

Rescue societies exist for every breed. If you don't feel you have the time or the temperament for a puppy or a kitten, why not adopt an older dog or cat that has already been trained? Visit your local animal shelter and consider taking in an animal that needs a good home. Adopting an older pet means you are likely to bring home an animal that is already house-trained. Puppies and kittens are like human newborns; they require a lot of extra attention the first year. You might not have the time, energy, or patience for this type of endeavor.

BE A RESPONSIBLE PET OWNER

There are millions of unwanted cats and dogs in the United States. Unless you're certain you will be breeding your pet, please be sure to have it spayed or neutered so you don't contribute to the pet overpopulation problem. Contrary to some beliefs, a spayed or neutered pet is actually a happier pet!

A few years ago I was in a pet store buying Katie some dog treats. Lo and behold they were having a sale on iguanas. I have always been fascinated by these exotic creatures and considered getting one. I could not believe they were only $15! Still, something told me *not* to make this an impulse purchase. After all, any pet is a living creature that deserves to be treated with respect.

I went home and called my best friend. Should I buy an iguana? The price was the big draw. Who can't afford $15? Susie suggested I research iguanas on the Internet before I brought one home. I am so glad I did! They are wonderful pets but require a lot of highly specialized care. They can also grow to six feet in just a few years!

What's the moral of the story? Research any pet you are thinking of making a member of your family. Cats, for example, come in a wide variety of breeds. Birds can be messy and noisy. Do your homework and your efforts will be richly rewarded.

THE GUEST ROOM

My mother taught me something that sums up the care of a guest room. She said, "Regina, when you go to someone's home, look carefully at the guest room. Memorize it. Then leave it exactly as you found it." Words to live by, don't you think? Of course when you are the hostess, the responsibility to create a room worthy of duplicating rests with you! Here are some guest room tips to make this room inviting to your family and friends:

- If you need to use the closet or the dresser drawers in this room for storage (and most people do), be sure you have at least one drawer and some closet space cleared for your guest. They will need some hangers as well for their clothes. Have these items in place. It isn't very welcoming to hear your hostess say, "Oh! I guess you will need some hangers, won't you? I'll go get them now."

- A friend of mine is a superior hostess. When I visit Binnie's home, I know that a carafe of fresh water and a glass will be on the nightstand. I also know that a tiny bouquet of fresh flowers from her garden will be in the guest bath. These tiny touches make me feel so welcome.

- Be sure that extra blankets and pillows are available. Nothing is worse than waking up cold in someone's house and not having a clue where the blankets are kept.

- Empty the trash can in the room and put in a fresh liner.

- Stock the bathroom with adequate toilet paper, fresh towels, and perhaps a guest robe. (This doesn't have to be one purchased expressly for guests. I am sure you can share one of yours.)

- Let your guests know that you have everyday items on hand for their use, such as shampoo, hair styling products, a hair dryer, toothpaste, and body lotion. It can mean a lighter suitcase for them—a special blessing if they're flying in to visit you.

- If you use this room on a daily basis because it doubles as your gym or home office, work out a schedule with your guest upon their arrival. This way you can perform your normal activities and they will have some guaranteed privacy.

AN EXTRA-WARM WELCOME

Make your overnight guests feel at home by keeping a small basket filled with sample-size toiletries such as bubble bath, soap, shampoo, and body lotion in the guest bath. It's a great way to use those travel sizes that we all accumulate!

FINAL NOTE

So often we make assumptions about various aspects of our future life with a partner. We feel that love will conquer all of our problems. Unfortunately, love is powerful but it is not a magic elixir. We need to communicate our thoughts, feelings, and personal philosophies about all the key areas of our lives openly, freely, and often. None is more important than how we wish to raise our children. If you have specific differences and are each bringing children into the home, it is ideal to work out compromise solutions before the families are blended. Our children are the most valuable legacy we live in this world. The family home you create for them shapes their future and influences the way they will raise their children. Their rooms are the training ground for the physical worlds they will create for themselves.

9

THE GARAGE, ATTIC, AND STORAGE UNITS

"A house should change. It should never stay static. If it does, it's symbolic of your life."

—Jasper Conran, designer

I can count on one hand the number of garages I have encountered over the years that were actually used for cars. I tell you this to relieve any sense of guilt you might have. If you haven't driven your car into the garage in a few years, you are in the majority. I do remember one garage that stands out as the most organized of all. It was on an estate. It was huge. In fact I think it held eight vehicles. It was carpeted and the walls had artwork on them. When I asked the owner why he went to all this trouble for a garage, he gave me a wonderful answer: "We are responsible for everything God sends to us. This is how I express my gratitude."

Let's dive right in with a bit of journaling so we can craft an immediate plan for this room. It is, after all, a part of the home, isn't it? Are you thinking it isn't worth the time and effort it would take to get it straightened out? Are you tempted to skip this and go directly into the next chapter and tackle your home office? Consider this: The last view of your home as you drive off to work or run errands and the first view of your home upon your return is the garage. Don't you think you would feel better if it were in order? Wouldn't it be nice to have it organized and housing all the things that do not belong in the home itself? I knew I could convince you!

WHAT'S GOING ON HERE?

Let's begin with a brief quiz. Please answer the following questions in your journal.

1. Are items stored in the garage because you either refuse to or cannot make a decision about their fate?
2. Has it been a long time since you checked the stuff stored in the garage to check its relevance to your current life?
3. Do you have a log of what is stored?
4. Are you keeping some things out of obligation? For example, have grown children saddled you with their memorabilia so they don't have to clutter their homes? Were you left things by a deceased relative and feel guilty even thinking about going through it all?
5. Has your partner usurped the majority of the available space?
6. Have you become the "space hog"?
7. Do you have sports items from the days when your kids were in school?
8. Are there items that represent fleeting interests like camping or skiing?
9. Can your car(s) fit into the garage?

10. Would you like to convert the garage for a specific or unique use? I have a client, for example, who turned the garage into a rehearsal space for her band. Her car is parked on the street, which in Southern California isn't an issue, weather-wise. What would you like to create?

If you could have the garage of your dreams, what would you store there? Here are the most common items (feel free to add your own):

◆ Car(s) and automotive products

◆ Sports equipment

◆ Tools

◆ Holiday decorations

◆ Bicycles

◆ Extra refrigerator or freezer

◆ Earthquake kit (pertinent in some areas only)

◆ Pantry shelves (overflow from house)

◆ Gardening supplies

◆ Cleaning tools (large brooms, mops, etc.)

◆ Lawn care equipment (mowers, gasoline, motor oil, etc.)

◆ _____

◆ _____

The garage is usually the domain of the man of the house. Very often this bothers his spouse. Ladies, just as a child needs some autonomy over his bedroom, a man very often needs to feel that some part of the home is under his control. If you have frilly lace in the bedroom, a pink powder room, and a leopard print sofa, let your husband organize the garage.

WORKABLE STORAGE SPACE

As elsewhere in the house, the garage should be organized by category. If anyone needs a tool, flowerpot, or extension cord, he shouldn't have to wait for Dad to come home from work to find out where he hid the item in question. The items should be easily accessible as well. The same goals we had in the home for our projects hold true here: The garage can be beautiful after it is organized. It should function easily so that you can always find what you need. And of course, it should be organized in such a way that new items have a logical place to live. Ready to proceed?

I want you to do a rough sketch of the floor plan of the garage. Mark off in pencil where you envision each category being located. Do you have enough space? Perhaps you won't be able to use the garage for your car. If you live in a temperate climate like Southern California, this isn't an issue. If you live in an area where the winters are brutal, it isn't a choice. Your car needs protection from the elements. What has to go? What's unrealistic on your part?

In addition to the garage, in this chapter we're taking into consideration outside storage—which can mean a storage unit on your property or the rental of space in a public storage facility—and the attic. These three spaces work in concert. If you have an attic, some of these categories are perfect for storage there instead of the garage. For example, holiday decorations would be an ideal candidate. Is there anything else that could go into the attic? Why not create a list so you can keep track of possessions that are to be given a new home? When we get out to the garage and begin putting our plan to work, please set those items aside. Later we'll take them to the attic.

If you have outside storage, please answer these important questions:

◆ Is your outside storage really necessary or an expensive luxury?

◆ Do you know what is currently stored there?

- Have you added up what you have spent to date on rental fees?
- Could that money be better spent for the needs of your family?
- When you go to the storage area, can you easily put your hands on whatever you need?

If your answers lead you to believe that outside storage is an invaluable resource for you, is there space for more items? What from your list could be transported to storage? Please put those items aside when we start work.

Now let's create a shopping list and gather our resources. Most people will need most of the following items for the big clean-up-the-garage day:

- Hooks to hang bicycles
- Shelving
- Sports equipment organizer
- Work bench/peg board/containers for small items like nails, etc.
- Heavy-duty trash bags
- A Dumpster for the day, if necessary
- Heavy-duty plastic containers (on wheels if possible)
- Portable containers on wheels with drawers (we've used these in the closet)
- Label maker with extra cassettes
- Sharpie permanent marker
- Water and healthy snacks for everyone
- Music, if it helps you work

You'll also want help moving some of the heavier items. Perhaps the teenage son of a neighbor or friend would like to earn a little extra money? Remember, however, that most men feel that the garage is their province. If you have such a man in the house, be sure to include him in the planning phase. He might even want to do all the physical hauling and lifting, eliminating the need for that borrowed teenager!

CHARITY BEGINS AT HOME

Book a charity to pick up large items. If you're no longer interested in a hobby (such as camping) or a sport (such as skiing) that requires specialized equipment, with one phone call you can secure space in your garage, give your languishing possessions a new lease on life, and take a tax deduction!

Let's follow the Magic Formula and see if we can't whip the garage into shape. Are you ready?

STEP ONE: ELIMINATE

By now you know where we start with all our projects. We *eliminate!* If you can clean the garage out on a nice, warm day, you'll be able to use the driveway as your extended work surface. You'll want to clean up quickly by dusk so the neighbors can't complain about the eyesore you created for the entire neighborhood. As you go through your items, keep your goal in mind. For most people, the goal will be to get the car(s) into the garage.

STEP TWO: CATEGORIZE

As you make your decisions, you will trash some items, donate others, set aside some for the attic, and set aside others for storage. Perhaps you'll want to organize a garage sale to sell some items. You will also create separate areas for the items that belong in the categories you agreed upon for the space. For example, you'll have a designated work space in the driveway for all the tools and another for any household items you are storing in the garage because the pantry is not adequate to the task. A long folding table is an invaluable tool for the day. If you don't have one, see if a neighbor or friend has one you can borrow!

STEP THREE: ORGANIZE

If you can, have your helper eliminate what you are trashing as soon as the final decisions have been made and the garage is ready to be organized. The absence of this debris will, as always, help you think more clearly. A stack of garbage will also indicate how far you have come in the process.

If your husband is helping, I am sure he will want to set up his workbench and his tools. I am equally certain he will not be remotely interested in the proper storage of the holiday ornaments. The garage is perhaps the one area where two can work simultaneously and actually make good progress.

Let's talk about some individual storage solutions.

HOLIDAY ORNAMENTS

Heavy-duty plastic bins are ideal for storing holiday ornaments. Not only do cardboard boxes wear out over time, they also provide instant food for rodents and critters. Year after year they get so shabby looking, it can be depressing to take out the ornaments! If you purchase these containers for your young child's toys, they can be used for storage later. They really do have more than one use, and that makes the price more economical over time.

With the holiday ornaments, I would wrap the largest items, like the holiday village or the manger, in the bottom container. Make this the large size on wheels. A medium-size container can sit on top of that housing all of the ornaments and balls wrapped in tissue paper. (In the following illustration the ornaments are not wrapped so you can see them.) On top of that you can place a small container filled with the holiday lights. When you want to haul out your ornaments from the bowels of the garage, attic, or storage locker, you can pull one container and have all three instantly at your command. Here is another use for your trusty label maker.

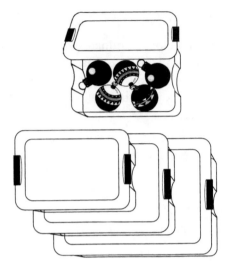

Storage chests of various sizes are good for organizing holiday ornaments.

BICYCLES

They are best stored off the ground on hooks, especially if inclement weather prevents you from using them every day. Be careful not to store them so high you need a crane to get them down.

SPORTS EQUIPMENT

Why not purchase a sports organizer to hold baseball bats, basketballs, skates, helmets, and other sports equipment? This is a storage rack that is specifically designed to hold all the accoutrements of the various sports that you fancy. But remember: If you no longer engage in a particular sport, pass along your equipment to someone who will appreciate it. You will automatically acquire more space for your current interests.

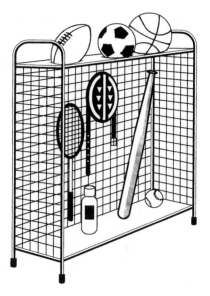

A sport station like this one organizes all your recreational equipment in one place.

TOOLS

If someone in the home is handy with tools, he will certainly want to have a workbench and tools in one area. In general, the person who is going to be using the tools should organize this area. That way he'll know where everything is. And if the time has passed for making things, the bench and extra tools can be donated to a charity.

A WELL-STOCKED TOOLBOX

Even if no one enjoys making things, it's still a good idea to have a well-stocked toolbox. You only need a few basic tools to be able to tackle most emergencies in the home. A sales person at your local home store will help you put together a toolbox.

NATURAL DISASTER PREPAREDNESS

Just about every area is prone to one kind of natural disaster or another. Here in Los Angeles, earthquake preparedness is important. You can contact a chapter of the Red Cross and see exactly what you need. One word of caution: Don't store your supplies in an area that will be difficult to reach in the event of a disaster.

SHELVES

Shelf space is the saving grace of any garage. If you can't afford to have a closet company come and create built-in storage cabinets, you can pick up some sturdy, inexpensive shelving units at your local home store. Ideally, each unit can house a particular category. For example, one unit might act as your extra pantry while another holds your automotive and earthquake needs and a third keeps your gardening supplies in order. The bottom line is that you don't want mounds of stuff, no matter how brilliant the category, piled around the garage. You want your floor space kept clear.

THE ATTIC

Whether your attic is a glorified crawl space or a large, secret room tucked into the top of your home, be sure you know what you have decided to keep in this bonus area. What do I mean? If you have a penchant for tossing boxes of stuff up there that you just know one day you will be ready to go through, you will have unfinished business hanging over your head.

Many years ago a lovely lady took my class. She was well into her 80s. I was curious about what prompted her to get organized so late in life. She told me she didn't want to leave a mess for her children. She wanted to set her affairs in order before she died. I hope I can open myself to learn new things when I am her age.

Shelf space in the garage is a must.

Don't let your inability to make a decision be the legacy you leave your children. Learning how to make decisions gets easier with practice. It really is a skill you can master. So many of my clients begin a session with me absolutely in awe that they can toss a piece of paper. By the time we're done, they have bags of unwanted papers ready to be tossed. Remember, too, that on a purely practical note, a stuffed attic with no rhyme or reason to its setup is a fire hazard.

By the way, here's a list of items you *don't* want to store in the attic:

◆ Perishables such as dry cereals, bread, and dry pet food. You don't want to inadvertently attract any unwanted critters like bugs or mice.

◆ Woolens such as blankets, sweaters, and coats. The concern here is, of course, moths.

◆ Items affected by extreme heat or cold such as leather goods, photographs, and wood furniture.

◆ Valuables such as jewelry, important papers, or cash. Place these in a fireproof home safe or safe-deposit box at your bank.

OFF-SITE STORAGE

This is usually a small room in a large facility. If you find you do need some storage away from the home, don't allow it to become a dumping ground. Plan what goes there and how it will be organized with the same care you did your closet or the garage. Here are some guidelines to assist you:

◆ Try to line at least one wall with some inexpensive, sturdy shelving units from the home store. This way your labeled boxes can be stacked and easy to retrieve when needed. Remember that categories should be created in this space. You don't want to stop by one day for your holiday ornaments and have to spend three hours because all your boxes have been tossed in without rhyme or reason.

◆ Please don't store antiques or sentimental, irreplaceable, or extremely valuable items.

◆ Keep an inventory of what is stored.

◆ Clean out this space on a regular basis. If you can live without these items year after year, are you sure you need to hold on to them?

◆ Check to see if your homeowner's policy covers these possessions. If not, see if your storage facility sells insurance. At the very least you would want to have replacement value in the event of a theft, flood, or fire.

◆ Our wonderful thick plastic bins are best used here because rodents and other critters won't be able to eat their way through.

THE OVERZEALOUS ORGANIZER

Mary is an astute businesswoman, a wonderful wife, and the mother of four. Her ability to organize any space or project is legendary. Her husband is the exact opposite. John doesn't care how his home is organized or what the kids are up to. He knows that Mary has total control in these areas. In a sense, he can be an observer in his home rather than an active participant. He spends long hours at work.

As a very sentimental person, John has difficulty parting with the treasures from his past. As a man of means, he elected to store his treasures in a storage facility. Mary would not stop hounding him. She found that storage unit a waste of money and energy. When I did a special project for them, they asked me what I thought about the storage situation. My response might surprise you.

On the surface it would, of course, be best for John to release the energy of the past by tossing items he will never need or use again. But it's also true that this work must be done when the individual is ready. Mary is something of a control freak. I sensed that John wanted a place where he could, in fact, say no to the control that was being exerted everywhere else in his life.

I suggested that he keep the storage unit until he felt ready to let those things go. I recommended to Mary that she let this issue go. By the way, over the years, John and I have worked on releasing some of his possessions. He has made remarkable progress. Like the baby chicks we met earlier, no one can do this work until he is ready. Getting organized is more than a physical activity. It is an emotional release as well. Be sure you respectfully allow your partner to work at his or her own pace.

FINAL NOTE

When you and your partner decide to organize your house, remember that every physical location you have stored objects counts as part of your home. We want everything to work in concert with our stated goals of increased peace and order in the home.

10

THE HOME
OFFICE

*"Nothing is so fatiguing as the
eternal hanging on of an uncom-
pleted task."*

—William James, American
philosopher

I would be hard pressed to say which space in the home is the most
difficult to share. I would, however, surely put the home office near
the top of my list. This chapter will have a twofold purpose and a
bonus application. We will discuss how to set up an office that supports your goals rather than one that sabotages your best efforts.
Once the physical setup is completed, the inner workings of an
office must be addressed. A beautiful office with no filing system,
for example, can only be photographed for a magazine. It cannot
help you achieve your goals.

The guidelines in this chapter will enable you to set up your
home office and any workspace you use. It will help the stay-at-
home mom or dad as much as it assists the corporate executive.

ASSESSING YOUR NEEDS

Let's begin with a quiz that will shed some light on your true needs. Please answer yes or no to the following questions:

1. Do you currently have a space that functions as the home office?
2. If yes, are you using it regularly?
3. Is it set up with everything you need (adequate size desk, comfortable chair, file cabinet, etc.)?
4. Does your office work spill over into other areas of the home (the dining room table, the kitchen counters, or the couch)?
5. Is your desk cleared off each evening?
6. Do you or your partner run a business from the home?
7. If not yet set up, will this space be used solely by one person?
8. Do you allow your children to play here or to do their homework?
9. Are other aspects of your life intruding on this space (does it do double duty as a guest room, craft room, gym, or storage area)?
10. Was regular use of this room interrupted by an event in your life (for example, the addition of a child, the passing of a loved one, a trip)?
11. Are you eager to establish a home office?
12. Are you intimidated by anything to do with an office? Be specific. Do you feel it's time to conquer this fear?

As I have noted previously, very often it isn't until we see things in black and white that we have a clear idea of our situation and where we are headed. In many ways, the person establishing a home office for the first time has a somewhat easier time. They are in virgin territory. Those with a history of home office inadequacies or shortcomings will be a bit tainted by past efforts.

I think a bit of journaling at this point will assist you further. Increased understanding and a well-crafted plan will make the time you are up on your feet putting it all together a breeze. Please answer the following questions in your journal.

1. What do you wish to accomplish in your home office? It really helps to have a clear idea. Do you want a private area to pay bills and write in your journal? Or do you wish to establish a home-based business and support your family?

2. What related steps are you willing to take to ensure success? Will you part with furniture that doesn't serve the purpose of the room? Is it reasonable to expect you will be able to invest in office furniture and supplies? Can some aspects of the room be shifted to other areas of the house? Where, for example, will you store things if this room has become a dumping ground? Where will guests sleep?

3. How will your life be different if you succeed? Very often we make an intellectual or emotion-based declaration of purpose and then set up the physical space so that the stated goal is almost impossible to achieve. Are you really interested in achieving your stated goals? Are you willing to do what is necessary?

Let me give you a common example of self-sabotage. Most of my clients with a home office/guest room combination set the room up to make their guests comfortable. I ask how often they entertain friends or relatives who stay overnight. No matter how frequently that is, it is never greater than the number of days the client will enter that room needing to work in an office capacity. We care more about the comfort of others than we do about our own success. Is this true of you? Why do you suppose that is? Are you ready to change?

THE LOVE BIRDS: A STUDY IN SHARING OFFICE SPACE

Artist Ernie Weckbaugh did the illustrations you see in this book. Ernie and his wife, Patty, run a home-based business called Casa Graphics. They helped me self-publish *The Zen of Organizing* before it was published by Alpha Books. I know them to be hardworking, ethical, and absolutely delightful.

Ernie and Patty are together 24 hours a day. They have been married more than 40 years and have had this work arrangement for more than 25 years. This couple always amazes me. When they leave my home, they automatically hold hands. At dinner they speak about each other like newlyweds. I have rarely seen such love and mutual respect between any two people. Ernie and Patty not only work and live in their home, they would be lost without each other.

Once day I asked them the secret of their work relationship. In addition to love and respect, they acknowledged that each has particular and unique strengths they bring to the table. Ernie, for example, is the artist while Patty is the bookkeeper. Ernie's mind is the artistic force while Patty's is in charge of the nuts and bolts of the operation. Rather than arguing over differences, they use their unique strengths to create a united front and run a successful business.

Here, then, are the key ingredients you need to make sharing your office space a success: love, respect, and an honest evaluation of strengths and talents. This advice might seem obvious, but it is rarely heeded. Most home offices just happen, as if placing a desk in a room is all that is required.

If you are going to share a space, be sure you understand *how* the room is to be used, *who* will use it, and establish a *schedule*. When I am in my office to write, for example, it would drive me insane to have my partner making social phone calls. Writing is a creative act and requires peace to accomplish. It would be comforting, on the other hand, to have someone I love here paying bills or responding to e-mail while I worked on articles or a book. Do you see the difference? Let me acknowledge that as an only child I grew up with a lot of solitude. It is the most comfortable scenario for me. If you are like me and your partner is the youngest of eight, your work habits and comfort zones may be different.

A MATTER OF COMPROMISE

To successfully share office space, you and your partner need to acknowledge the differences in your work habits and come to a compromise. As creatures of habit, we often believe the way we've always done something is the only way possible. Compromise introduces us to new ways of doing and behaving.

By the way, if one of you is naturally tidy and the other has a desk that looks like a bomb went off, don't argue over this, please! Yes, being tidy will help anyone think more clearly and feel better about tackling the work on his or her desk. Getting organized is a personal journey, however, and not a result that can be forced on another human being. Teach by your example. And do try to discover what is *really* behind the irritation. I am going to bet it isn't stacks of paper on a desk. Now if these stacks include bills that never get paid, the issue is a matter-of-fact one. The person who can maintain the good credit of the family should be the one who handles the bill-paying task, not necessarily the one who desires to do it but can't quite get it done.

Let's address some practical issues. Are you ready to work on the physical setup of your home office?

THE PHYSICAL SPACE

If possible, try not to place your desk directly in line with the door as you enter the room (see the following illustrations). You want to be able to look up and easily see whoever enters. In feng shui this position of power applies even if you live alone. It's best if your back is not to the door. This very often happens when one leaves the writing surface of the desk and works on the computer.

You will be impacted and potentially weakened by the energy of everyone walking the halls outside your office. This is most prevalent in corporations, but applies at home as well. Let's face it—not everyone is happy at all times. If someone is sad, angry, or sick, you'll be impacted on a subtle level by that energy as the person walks toward you.

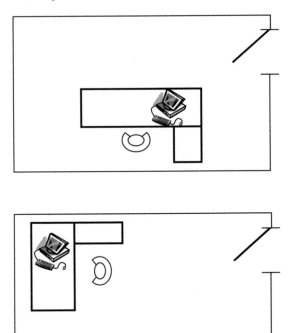

In the power position (top), your back is never to the door and you can easily see who is entering the room. In the weak position (bottom), your back is to the door, placing you in a more vulnerable position.

If you position your desk in accordance with these ancient feng shui principles, no matter what your belief system, I promise you will instantly feel more powerful and in control if you can look up and see whoever is entering your office. Why not try an experiment: Move your desk and see if you feel any differently. I had one client who steadfastly refused to move her desk. I finally convinced her to experiment. She sat down in the new position and exclaimed, "I feel like a captain of the industry!" See how it makes you feel!

If you can't move your desk, hang a mirror on the wall at eye level so you can look up and instantly see who is entering.

KEEP IT NEAT

Afraid that too many cords, wires, and cables will show if you move your desk? At your office supply store, buy a long tube in white or black that is made for the purpose of gathering and covering these items.

Where are you going to keep your office supplies? You would be surprised how many people have their supplies scattered about the home. You need to have everything at your fingertips. Most home offices are converted bedrooms. Why not convert the closet into a supply closet? You can put braces on the wall and lay boards across, creating storage shelves. You can just as easily place an inexpensive bookcase in the closet. Use those shelves for storage.

The supplies you need will be dictated by the type of business you conduct, but here's a list of the most basic items:

- Plain white paper for printer/copy/fax machine
- Toner and/or inkjet cartridges
- Pens and pencils (plus refills, if automatic)
- Pencil sharpener
- Stapler and staples

- Paper clips
- Tape dispenser and extra rolls of tape
- Scissors
- Correction fluid (such as Liquid Paper)
- Scratch paper and self-stick notes
- Sharpies and highlighters
- Binders, tabs for binders, and sheet protectors
- Label maker (of course!)
- File folders (manila and possibly one or two colors)
- Hanging file folders and long tabs for hanging files
- Bookends
- Magazine holders
- Drawer liners
- Box-bottom hanging files with a two-inch base

Here's a list of basic office equipment:

- Computer (desktop and/or laptop) and monitor
- Printer
- Scanner
- Fax machine
- Copy machine

Basic office furniture includes the following:

- Desk with a large working surface and a comfortable chair
- Vinyl pad under chair if on a carpet
- Worktable
- Bookcase
- File cabinet(s)
- Clock
- Desk lamp

In terms of room décor, here's what's nice to have:

♦ Good overhead lighting

♦ Carpeting or area rugs, or a folding screen to establish differ-ent zones in the room (work vs. reading, etc.)

Although they don't fall under the category of décor per se, painting the walls and washing the windows are examples of the actions you take when your self-esteem is high and you *really* want to succeed. You need to address every aspect of your home office to enhance the possibility of success. I guarantee most people won't think of these things. But once they get done, you will feel better ... and do them by instinct in the future.

It takes more than the right furniture to create a successful home office. It takes attention to detail. I am reminded of cooking: The best ingredients don't necessarily make the most delicious dish. It's the delicate contribution of the spices that move it to the winner's circle. Likewise, small touches in your office like the fol-lowing can make a big difference:

♦ Weekly fresh flowers or silk arrangements

♦ Plants

♦ Colorful artwork or posters on the wall that inspire you

Welcome the preparation of this room and the work you have to accomplish there as you might prepare for the arrival of a treas-ured guest. Be grateful to have work and the space to perform the necessary functions it requires. If you resent what you have to accomplish that energy will pervade the room and make working here less than a satisfactory experience. Not enough can be said for the power of an "attitude of gratitude."

A PERSONAL TRANSFORMATION

When I first moved to California from New York, I had no idea I would ever need a home office. I was lucky enough to have a spare room I turned into the most adorable guest room you have ever seen. The one thing that always saddened me was the fact that this room was so rarely enjoyed. Just big enough for a bed, a nightstand and a dresser, there was no way to make it a multipurpose room. I would peer in occasionally and regret how underutilized this space was and I longed to be able to enjoy it myself.

When I established my organizing business, it quickly became apparent that my guests would have to sleep in the living room and the guest room would have to be turned into an office. I had tried working as I sat on the couch and watched TV. I had a portable file case that was beautiful to look at but not adequate for the files it takes to run a business. Making the commitment to physically change the character of my guest room helped solidify my stated goals for my business.

We succeed in direct proportion to the respect we pay the goals we say we wish to accomplish. As my mother used to remind me all the time, "Talk is cheap!"

Let's examine some of the specific items you'll be using in this room that can enhance your ability to succeed. You might not have all these, but you'll certainly want to invest in as many as you can.

THE DESK

You'll want a desk that allows you a writing area, as well as space for your computer. In other words, you need a surface for tasks like hand writing thank you notes and paying your bills, as well as an area for your monitor and keyboard. Flat screen monitors are coming down in price and are desirable because they take up less room. Don't break the bank, however, over an aesthetic choice. A regular monitor will do just fine. We all have our wish lists, right?

If you want to save money and you have the space, you can buy an unfinished simple door at the local home store. Have the store put a stain on the door or do it yourself. Your unfinished door now looks like the expensive wood of your choice and will match the furniture you have for the room. Place the door on two two-drawer file cabinets, and voilà! A desk is born! You can feed the wires from your equipment through the door handle opening. Clever, isn't it? Do you remember the famous rolling cart that we have used throughout the house? Position one behind you to take the place of the desk drawers you don't have with this arrangement.

It's best if you have a good-quality light on the desk and a light behind you that shines onto the work surface. You will be miserable if you can't see clearly what you are working on. Keep your drawers organized by category. You don't want to have to rifle through things to find a simple item like a paper clip. You want to know where your paper clips are and that you have extras in your supply closet/area. The drawer liner and small containers you used in the kitchen and bathroom to keep order in these hidden areas will work beautifully to organize your desk drawers.

INFORMATION AT YOUR FINGERTIPS

Bulletin boards are useful for keeping important phone numbers, business cards, reminders, supply lists, and other notes within easy view. Just remember to keep it tidy so it's not covered with papers! If wall space is limited, use a three-ring binder with sheet protectors for your most frequently accessed information. Label it "Reference" and keep it handy.

FILES

You will need several types of files in your office. Let's look at the types and the ideal placement for each category. Then, for those who need it, we'll review the steps to follow to set up a working file system. You won't be surprised to know it involves the Magic Formula, will you?

TYPES OF FILES AND THEIR LOCATION

The collected information that was once pertinent to your everyday life and will now rarely, if ever, be accessed should go in an *archival file*. This might include old tax returns, cancelled checks, and old bank or investment statements. If you have a garage, place a large file cabinet here and store this information. Lacking a garage, keep these files in clearly labeled boxes. Store them in your attic or at the top of the office closet on a shelf. Remember, though, that "rarely accessed" doesn't mean "dead zone." You will need to clean out these files periodically, ideally once a year.

Let me give you a classic example of archival files. We all need to keep our income tax returns forever. We need to keep the backup materials (the receipts for the items deducted on the tax return) for each return for a specified amount of time. (Please check with your tax representative to see what they recommend for you.) Each year as I file my current tax return, I toss the appropriate backup material. Obviously, if you file a short form and have no deductions, you have no backup materials!

Every profession, including homemaker, comes with materials that one might need from time to time. These might include home-owner's warranties, apartment lease agreement, home escrow papers, and information specific to your profession. Real estate agents might, for example, have files on city laws and ordinances, old marketing samples, and so on. These *reference files* should be kept in an area by themselves. The best place would be a file drawer labeled "Reference." I would prefer to see you have material in your desk drawer files that are in almost constant use like current projects. Reference materials are best kept in a file cabinet you either keep in your supply closet or near your desk.

You'll want to keep some items like your bills and personal correspondence as *personal files,* separate from the materials that represent your business life. This is exactly like keeping your casual clothes separate from your business suits in a closet.

Every profession has related materials. These *work files* can be sorted by category and turned into files that keep critical information at your fingertips. Let's take the example of a real estate agent. This is one of those professions that is top heavy with paper.

Lawyers and doctors face similar challenges. With real estate, you could have every bit of information in a file and arrange it alphabetically. Your fingers, however, will be doing an awful lot of walking with this system!

It would be better to divide your information into categories and have each category kept in alphabetical order. Samples of categories for real estate professionals include marketing, listings, escrows, information for sellers and buyers, and general real estate information (zoning, vendors, and office policies).

Action files are those you want at your fingertips. You can keep them in a separate drawer or on your desk in a portable file container. In this area I suggest you include the following categories:

- Calls
- To Do
- Bills: To Pay
- To File

You might want to designate these files a special color so that they always stand out on your desk.

TIPS FOR A PERFECT FILE SYSTEM

A file system is meant to be a collection of materials that help you to be more productive, not a near incoherent gathering of miscellaneous materials. Let's take a look at how the Magic Formula can once again come to our rescue:

1. No matter how many stacks of paper you have, even if you haven't seen the floor in years, remember: The whole of anything is very often overwhelming. It's easier to narrow your focus to just one stack at a time. Once you have that stack before you, your focus will narrow further. One paper at a time is all you have to deal with.

   Be sure you have a nice, clean work area. You'll want to have a good-quality garbage bag at your side and a sharp pair of scissors. If you no longer need the paper in your hand, toss it. This is the time to eliminate everything in your home office that no longer serves you or is needed. If you do want to hold on to it, what is it a part of? Now you will make stacks on your worktable that will be related to one another. You might, for example, have stacks of categories that include bills, recipes, travel articles, warranties, and tax receipts.

When it comes to newspaper and magazine articles, if you really do need the information, cut out the article and toss the excess. If you have a copy machine, make a copy and file that instead of the original. Plain paper doesn't disintegrate as quickly as newspaper or magazines.

Once everything is sorted you will have eliminated and categorized. Now it's time to organize your treasures.

SPACE HOGS

If you have a scanner, don't fool yourself into believing that a scanned article (or digital photographs, for that matter) isn't taking up valuable space on your hard drive. You might want to keep this kind of information on disks or burn it onto CD-ROMs. This will keep your computer running at full speed.

2. You'll need to assemble your stacks of materials into appropriate files. I like to use manila folders for everyday business like bills and designate colored folders for specific projects. As examples, my materials for this book are in blue folders and my marketing materials are in red. Feel free to be creative and choose the colors that please you. Be sure to label each file folder with your label maker. This creates an easy-to-read, uniform, and calming effect in the file drawer. As you make your file folders, leave them in front of the area where they will be housed.

3. Now we're going to use one of two kinds of hanging file folders to complete the process. I wouldn't bother to

purchase these in color, by the way, as the extra expense isn't necessary. Color folders will be enough for our purposes. I would also avoid accordion folders unless you are saving lots of small receipts. The accordion files do expand but they never hold a series of folders as easily as a simple box-bottom hanging folder with the cardboard insert at the bottom.

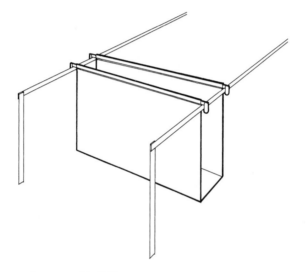

Box-bottom hanging file folder.

Let's look at a sample category to see how this works. Let's say you want to create a category called "Travel." This is going into the reference area, because you save articles for one big trip per year. When you're ready to select an area and plan your trip, you don't want to have to sort through a cardboard box filled with newspaper and magazine clippings. You'll want everything organized so that the process of choosing a vacation spot is enjoyable.

You would start by dividing your travel articles into areas of the world. Use a single hanging folder for each individual file or country. If an area of the world has several countries that interest you, you may need a box-bottom hanging folder to keep your category together and give you more space in the drawer. This might mean, for example, that you have eight countries in the folder marked "Europe." This is the big category under "Travel" and goes into a box-bottom folder. Be sure to keep both the hanging files and the individual folders in box-bottom folders in alphabetical order.

This section would look like this in the drawer:

Travel:

1. Africa (This is a continent, but perhaps you're considering a safari in South Africa. The only material you have relates to this activity in this one country.)

2. Europe (You might be leaning toward a trip to Europe but unable to narrow down the countries you wish to visit.)

   Denmark

   England

   France

   Germany

   Ireland

   Italy

   Sweden

   Switzerland

3. Middle East (Here again, you may only have an interest in one area, such as Egypt. Now, if you have two countries you want to visit—say, Egypt and Morocco—you will still place them in alphabetical order in a single hanging folder. Why not a box-bottom folder? Because without enough files to weigh it down, a box-bottom folder will pop up in the drawer. This will defeat your purpose because it will in fact be taking up more room.)

4. New Zealand

I like to use the extra long tabs to identify a hanging folder. Your label maker will create a visually beautiful display for the drawer. I don't like to stagger these tabs; an even row of tabs is much easier to read. In addition, if you permanently remove a file, you are going to suddenly have an uneven line.

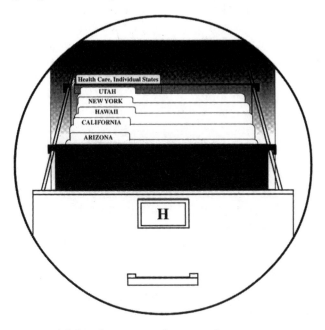

For easier readability, keep your tabs in one line.

GETTING USED TO THE NEW SYSTEM

It takes a few days to get used to a new setup. You might want to put your system on the computer and print out a copy. You can then pop the pages into sheet protectors and place them in a binder marked "Reference." You can keep all the information you need during the course of a day at your fingertips. For instance, in a large corporation this is the ideal place to keep your phone extension log. In the case of your files, it allows your fingers to literally do the walking and search for a file. This saves you steps, which translates into time saved.

Once you have your file system computerized, remember to log in new files and delete old ones. This again is time well spent.

If you get to the point where you want to hire an assistant, learning your file system will be a snap. They do not have to open and close a series of drawers. They need only read a few pages of reference materials. If you find yourself unable to keep up with the amount of material that needs to be filed, consider hiring a part-time assistant. Your local college is a great source. You might also want to call your local place of worship and see if they might know a retired person who would enjoy working one day a week. There is always a way to make life easier if we are willing to ask for help.

BOOKCASES

Bookcases, of course, are the ideal place for books related to the work you do, as well as other items. I can't imagine your guests want to see marketing books in the living room or the family room. No matter where your books are, be sure the arrangement of the bookcase is pleasing to the eye. Everywhere you look in your home you want to be instantly brought back to a sense of peace and calm. The next time you're on the phone arguing for a refund, it will make you feel better just to look up and see a family photo on the bookcase. Don't forget to use bookends to hold your books upright. Books that have tumbled into a heap on the shelf do nothing to bring a sense of peace to your environment!

THE MULTIPLE-USE ROOM

If your office needs to double as a guest room or workout room, remember to keep related items in one area. Try not to have a huge bed in this room. Instead, offer your guests a comfortable couch (perhaps one that unfolds into a bed) or a futon. The new inflatable beds set up in seconds, thanks to attached motors, and can be stored in a closet when not in use. If you have a gym in the room, keep the equipment in one area of the room. Use folding screens and area rugs to mark off the activity zones in the room just as you did elsewhere in the home.

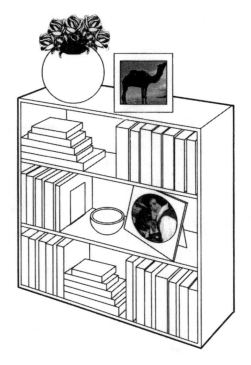

Bookcases are indispensable in most any room.

CRAFTING A LIFE

There's little point in getting organized if you don't know where you want to go in life. What if you had a new car, a full tank of gas, and no destination? You might never leave the driveway! Your organized home will better enable you to achieve your goals. Because many of our goals fall into the career aspects of our lives, let's take a break in our office organizing to look at how to manage our time. After all, once you get organized, you'll want to understand how to make use of all that time you've spent fretting about your chaotic environment!

Let's begin with an exercise in your journal. Please take five minutes to write down what you want to achieve in the next year. Remember your life is divided into many areas, such as family, work, friends, spiritual, and education. Be sure you address all of them. Here are two examples to get you started.

Journal Entry: Achievements for Coming Year

Family: Help son improve in math, work on relationship with step-daughter, take a romantic vacation with husband

Work: Get promotion, improve new skills, take advanced training classes

Friends: Set up more girls' nights out, arrange play dates for son

Spiritual: Go to church more often, help with ladies auxiliary, work with youth group

Education: Take French class, attend quilting seminar

Journal Entry: Achievements for Coming Year

1. After getting my home organized, I will have more time to devote to my family and career. In one year, the final papers for my Master's degree will be completed. I have been delaying this for some time and am now ready to enjoy this achievement.

2. With the house in order, I'll be able to schedule exercise into my weekly routine. This always makes me feel better! I will start a walking group in my neighborhood. On days the weather prevents us from walking, I will use the treadmill. My goal is 12 miles a week.

3. John and I need time away from the kids. Once I am organized, we can actually schedule a getaway. It's important to keep our relationship strong. The kids are getting older and will be leaving for college soon. John and I used to love to explore bed & breakfasts along the coast when we were dating. I'll be sure and schedule at least one weekend a year at a new B&B!

If your spouse does the same exercise, it will be interesting to compare notes. You might be unconsciously headed in two different directions. This might turn into a good time for what a friend of mine calls "a mid-course correction." Once you complete this exercise, please return to this chapter. I would prefer that you not read on until you have your exercise in hand.

Few people direct their lives with choices and goal setting. Their lives unfortunately just seem to "happen" to them. A sea of requests from other people and organizations carries them along from day to day. Indeed these requests are often interpreted as demands one cannot turn down. Life can, however, absolutely be directed to achieve your life purpose. In fact it is our right and a duty. How? By understanding that time is a commodity like money or food. You do quite literally use it or lose it.

If you don't have a daily planner, it should be your first purchase whether your office is a separate room in your home, the corner office in a corporate tower, or a few days a month spent sitting at the kitchen table paying bills. Want to work on organizing your home? Schedule the time as you might lunch with a dear friend. Do you do grocery shopping? Are your children in after-school activities? Would you like to work more on PR and see your business grow? You need to plot a course, and your calendar will help you do it.

Now I have another exercise for you. I'd like to you look at the current week in your planner or make a calendar page in your journal. It doesn't have to be fancy. Draw a square that covers one page. Draw lines that divide the pages into the days of the week. Now fill in the activities that comprise a typical week. Take a look at the following example.

When you're done, please continue to read.

One Week Calendar

MONDAY	TUESDAY
Make breakfast	Make breakfast
Make kids' sack lunch	Make kids' sack lunch
Take kids to school	Take kids to school
Go to work	Go to work
Pick up kids at school	Pick up kids at school
Make dinner	Make dinner
Homework with kids	Homework with kids
Exercise	Pay bills
WEDNESDAY	**THURSDAY**
Make breakfast	Make breakfast
Make kids' sack lunch	Make kids' sack lunch
Take kids to school	Take kids to school
Go to work	Go to work
Pick up kids at school	Pick up kids at school
Make dinner	Make dinner
Homework with kids	Homework with kids
Read book	Exercise
FRIDAY	**SATURDAY**
Make breakfast	Make breakfast
Make kids' sack lunch	Kids' soccer game
Take kids to school	Picnic lunch with kids
Go to work	Clean house
Pick up kids at school	Exercise
Dinner at restaurant	Family dinner
	SUNDAY
	Make breakfast
	Go to church
	Family lunch
	Do laundry
	Wash car
	Homework with kids
	Make dinner

PLOTTING YOUR COURSE

One of the most frequent questions I am asked is, "How do I write a book?" The first step is obvious: Sit down and start writing. As soon as you have a few chapters completed, take them to an editor. In addition to writing, one must research one's topic. What is already out there in the market place on this subject? How is your take on this information valuable? And most critical of all perhaps, who is your targeted audience?

Most of the time, the more information I give, the more blank the stare I see before me. It is human nature to want things to be easy. Sitting at a computer writing a book sounds like an easy job, doesn't it? It is actually one of the most physically, emotionally, and spiritually draining experiences you can have.

What does this story have to do with your calendar and plotting your course through life? Just about everything. Take a minute now to read your one-year goals, then study your calendar week. Is there any relation between what you say you want to achieve and what you are actually doing with your life on a day-to-day basis? More often than not my students are shocked to see very little relation at all. Life is created by our choices and our actions. Our good intentions are like the prologue to a good book. They might be interesting, but they aren't the heart of the matter.

FINAL NOTE

Our homes provide a sanctuary from the world. Our home offices are where we create the environment that encourages and supports our best efforts to achieve the higher purpose of our lives. Whether you are a stay-at-home parent or the president of the United States, your contribution is part of the mosaic of life. When we all contribute our unique gifts, we are the ultimate orchestra playing in time.

11

CREATING A SACRED SPACE

*"When we come to a point of rest
in our own being, we encounter a
world where all things are at rest,
and then a tree becomes a mystery,
a cloud becomes a revelation, and
each person we meet a cosmos
whose riches we can only glimpse."*

—*Dag Hammarskjöld, Swedish
statesman*

There are many healing modalities one can use to turn the home into a sacred space. Central to all is the creation of an organized environment. When chaos reigns over a home, the feeling or energy in the home is one of upset. It is in the extreme, like living in a boat that is constantly being tossed about in a storm on the high seas. Does this capture the feeling in your home?

No one ever promised that living with other human beings was going to be easy. Indeed it seems that the average relationship becomes more of an opportunity to work out our psychological and emotional issues than a situation that invites solace, doesn't it? The conscious creation of a sacred space can do much to change the established patterns in the home. Peace can replace warfare. Ease and comfort can replace upset. The way is open for love to fill the home.

We're going to briefly consider ways several world traditions bless the home. I invite you to explore your ethnic heritage, as well as your spiritual tradition for personal assistance you can most easily relate to. Catholic priests came to homes in Brooklyn when I was a child to sprinkle holy water and impart a blessing. Jews had a mezuzah on the door and touched it as they entered. The neighborhood of my childhood was alive with personal ways of showing reverence for the home. What lies in your background that will comfort your soul and bless your home?

My choice to invite the creation of a sacred space has been to follow the teachings of the Black Hat School of Feng Shui. (It's pronounced *fung schway* and means means "wind and water.") This is where we will begin our journey to the sacred.

FENG SHUI: THE CHINESE ART OF PLACEMENT

The Chinese believe that chi, or energy, is what fills the universe. Energy can become encapsulated in one place. Let's look at the human body. Here is an encapsulation of energy we can all relate to! When the doctor of traditional Chinese medicine uses acupuncture needles, the theory is that blocked energy is released to flow again. Blocked energy is also described as stagnation of chi and an invitation for disease to begin.

Your home is another easy-to-see encapsulation of energy. In fact, feng shui has taught for thousands of years that the unique energy of your home wishes to support you in achieving the purpose for which you have been born. It is modern man with his proliferation of magazines, newspapers, electronic toys, junk mail, and all manner of personal "stuff" who has clogged the flow of energy in his personal living space. Just as the acupuncturist releases energy with a needle, so to the professional organizer releases stagnation in the home or office by eliminating piles and stacks of stuff from desks, behind doors, the floor, countertops, closets, and furniture. You can function as your own professional organizer by using the guidelines in this book.

There are, by the way, two major schools of feng shui. One is the traditional Chinese Compass School and the other is the Black Hat School. They both use the same diagram, called the bagua, which you'll learn about in a moment. The Compass School, as the name implies, uses the directions of the compass for placement of objects in the home and indeed of the home itself on its plot of land.

The Black Hat School, founded by Professor Lin, uses the bagua exclusively. With this diagram as my guide, I can enter the front door of any home and know instantly which parts of the home govern specific aspects of life. My next step is to stand in the door of each individual room in the home and see how those areas of life are now being affected by the setup of that space. We could say this is examining the macro- and the microcosm of the house to achieve maximum flow of positive energy. Are you a little confused? These are new and therefore strange concepts and unfamiliar words. Let's see if I can't make this a little more concrete for you.

A word of caution is due at this point. It is impossible to reduce the art of feng shui to a few pages. Volumes have been written about this sacred philosophy for thousands of years. If you go to your local bookstore, you will probably find an entire section filled with feng shui books. (Check the appendix at the end of this book for a few to get you started.) Our goal here is to get a rudimentary understanding of this ancient art. This will enable you to ask your feng shui practitioner more intelligent questions and to easily grasp what he or she is doing in and for your home.

THE ANCIENT ROAD MAP

The bagua, shown in the following figure, is the diagram used by both of the main schools of feng shui. Here is a quick way to grasp how it works. In your journal draw a rough sketch of the floor plan of your home. Pretend that you are looking down on it from an angle above. I can't draw at all but I can pencil in a simple square. The average home is basically a box, so this is all that is required. Mark off the different rooms in the home. (If you live in an apartment, by the way, your floor plan is what we're after. I will use the word *home* to represent either a house or an apartment.)

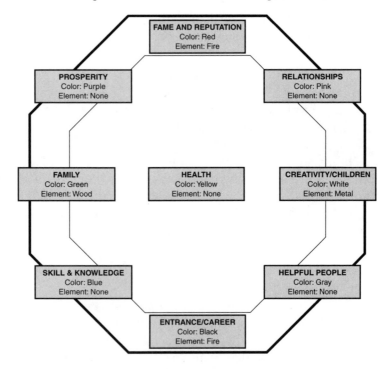

The bagua.

Please make a copy of the bagua you see here on tracing paper. It's basically a square with the corners cut off! Be sure to write in the same colors, elements, and areas of life noted on the diagram. As you lay the bagua over the sketch of your floor plan, you will see that different areas of your home govern certain aspects of your life. Moreover, all areas have designated colors and some have specific elements noted as being significant.

The front door of the home or the main entrance to each room is always the bottom of the bagua. The color is black and the area of life governed here is career. This is the entry point whether you are examining a home or an individual room. This main entrance is called "the mouth of the chi" or the place where energy enters the space. By the way, for those of you who enter your home via the garage, please use the front door of your home for our purposes. There is only one main entrance. Are you ready to continue?

Let's examine one area of the bagua and see how we use the indicated color and element for that area to enhance our life experience. The main entrance to your home is a wonderful place to begin. If you haven't had a chance to get organized, what do you see there? Have boots, hats, and gloves spread out onto the entry floor from the hall closet? Does mail get stacked up on the entry table and forgotten? Do your children drop school bags here and run? You get the idea.

This area in feng shui influences your career. Could we say that the state of your career is accurately depicted in this chaotic scene? Are you in flux career wise? Or perhaps this entrance is devoid of decoration and appears untouched and neglected. Do you see the messages we look for in the space that tell us about the related aspect of the client's life experience?

The first step in enhancing your career through feng shui would be not so much to "tidy up" but to create a *system* in this area that will handle the activities and keep everything under control for the future. Here is a classic example of the difference between a quick tidy up and creating a system. Suppose my dining room table has become my desk. I decide to restore the table to its original purpose and create a filing system that will handle not only what is stacked on the table today but all of the related materials that naturally flow in during the course of a day. If I become sick or have to travel, I might find a pile or two has reappeared. I have only, however, to schedule the time to work my system and restore order.

On the other hand, suppose I become demoralized and depressed by the piles on my dining room table and toss everything into a box. I swear that one day soon I am going to deal with all of it. In the meantime, however, the box gets shoved into a closet. The room looks tidy and inviting to company, but nothing constructive has been done to handle either what was there or what will follow. This is the essential difference between a quick tidying up and creating a system. You want the latter established in every area of your home whether or not you decide to employ any feng shui concepts.

By the way, organizing and feng shui go hand in hand. In the following illustration you see a large table that fits perfectly in an entry. You can leave your keys in the harvest basket as you enter. There are drawers for storage and areas for display. This table is at once useful and decorative. You might hang a black shelf with ceramic fish as a way of introducing the water element. I hung a bagua mirror over the table to invite increased energy flow to the careers of the occupants. Just imagine, in addition to function and feng shui, you can also primp as you head out the door!

A hall table with a bagua mirror above it works well in the entry.

SOMETHING'S FISHY!

Have you ever noticed that most Chinese restaurants have a large fish tank near the main entrance? Rather than a love of fish, this is classic feng shui. Remember the bagua suggests water in this area. Water represents money. The fish keep the water moving which increases the flow of money into the home or place of business.

Rest assured you do not have to install a large fish tank in the entrance to your home. But this is the perfect place for a small water fountain. Because the color for this area is black, you would ideally place your fountain on a black stand. Metal also represents water, so a black wrought iron stand would be ideal. (As an aside, choose your fountain carefully. Some splash water and others are very noisy. You might inadvertently encourage your family members to have to visit the bathroom more frequently!)

You might feel that there is too much activity in this area for an actual water fountain. Water is key in this area. How you introduce it is a matter of taste. What about framed pictures or paintings of water scenes? Do you like dolphins? What about an old sailing ship out on the ocean? However you choose to represent the element of water in your entryway, make sure the scene is calm. You don't want to introduce the destructive possibilities of water into your career!

Continue to travel section by section first through the house as a whole and then through each room. Have you just naturally done some feng shui? Are there things you see you need to change immediately? One of my clients had her cat box in the prosperity corner of her home office! You can imagine the metaphor. See how you can creatively add the appropriate feng shui colors and, where appropriate, the indicated elements.

HIDDEN COLORS

Colors need not be seen to be effective. They can be hidden. How? Trace a bagua on construction paper in the color indicated for the area and hide it behind a picture frame, under a table, or behind a sofa cushion!

UNIFYING BODY, MIND, AND SOUL WITH FENG SHUI

Frequently a discussion of feng shui will cause someone to say rather angrily something along these lines: "Well, I brought one of those lucky bamboo plants home and nothing happened! That feng shui stuff doesn't work." My reply is always the same: "Are you really surprised it didn't work?" This is the feng shui equivalent of bringing home a treadmill, never using it, and complaining that you didn't lose any weight! This is what they call in therapy "magical thinking." There are no easy fixes.

There are three aspects to our lives: the physical, the mental, and the spiritual (or body, mind, and soul). When they work in concert, we perform at our optimum. And so do the feng shui "cures" we place in our environments.

In our previous example, someone hears that a bamboo plant is good luck in feng shui. He brings home a plant and plops it down, waiting for the magic to happen. The first consideration we need to have concerns the *physical* or body placement of this object. What area of life did you wish to enhance? Money? Referring once again to the bagua, the bamboo would go into your prosperity corner or into the career area (your home's entrance). Did you want to attract a relationship? Everything should be in twos in that area, so you might place two plants in your relationships corner.

After you pick the physical place, remember to check with your florist to see what the optimum conditions are for your plant. If you don't water it and place it where it is not likely to thrive, the feng shui consequences will not be positive. You are asking for more from your bamboo plant than just an attractive addition to your décor. I suggest you be respectful. With the proper placement, you have taken care of the body aspect. With its physical placement, your feng shui object is working for you at one-third power or, as my feng shui Master Nate Batoon likes to say, "chi watts."

Next we move on to the *mental* or mind aspect of this placement. As you place the bamboo in the career area to help boost your career, pause for a minute and do a brief visualization. Picture what the consequences of more energy in your career looks like. Be specific. This will boost your chi watts to two-thirds.

Finally, it's time to acknowledge the *spiritual* or soul aspect of this placement and your request. Do this by reciting the preferred Black Hat Sect prayer, "Om Mani Padme Hum" (an ancient mantra from Tibetan Buddhism), the prayer of your choice, or by simply uttering "Thank you." Your bamboo plant is now working at full power to assist you.

FENG SHUI CURES

Because we cannot cover this practice in depth, I thought I'd give you some tips and common cures for different areas of your home. You can employ these while you are searching for the right feng shui book or practitioner for your continued studies. We are going to proceed room by room.

THE BATHROOM

The bathroom is a place of drainage in the home. As my feng shui master Nate Batoon likes to say: "Let the waste go down but the energy rise." You might want to use some of the following feng shui tips in your bathroom:

- At the local hardware store you can pick up red electrical tape. Cut a nine-inch piece (nine is the power number in feng shui). Wrap this around the pipe under your sink. Wrap in one place like a Band-Aid, not running the length of the pipe. This stops the flow of excess money out of the home or office.

- Place some unpopped popcorn in a container with a lid on the back of the toilet tank. Fill it three-quarters full. This will symbolize that more energy is always available to you! You can also use a nine-inch strip of red ribbon and tie a bow around the container. Red, like black, is an activating color in feng shui, and nine is the most significant number. This extra boost will further energize household members. This is especially important when anyone is sick and visiting the bathroom frequently.

- If you have a window in the bathroom, hang a plant or place one in the window.

- In the absence of a window, hang a chime in this room. Chimes and plants breathe extra life and energy into any room.

- Use the appropriate feng shui color either on the walls, the decorative items, or the towels in the bathroom.

You can use these cures in all the bathrooms of your home. If you are concerned about your guests (or employees, in an office situation), remember that the only cure that will draw attention to itself is the popcorn. Even then, you needn't explain that this is a feng shui "cure." People will simply think you are creative in your decorating style! One of my doctors has this in her office bathroom and rarely do any patients ask what it signifies.

THE KITCHEN

No matter where it falls in the bagua, this room is associated with the flow of money into the home. Here are some fun things to increase your finances:

◆ Place a large dollar amount of fake bills on the refrigerator with a magnet. (This is the one magnet I think is appropriate on the refrigerator.) I have $9 million fanned out on mine. The magnet holding it in place is a New York City police officer! This represents "cold, hard cash."

◆ Plants in a window or on the kitchen table are a lovely touch that will increase the chi in this room. It's also a great place for an herb garden.

◆ Each stove burner represents 25 percent of your income. Be sure they are clean and in working order!

◆ Place a small bagua mirror above the burners to reflect them and increase your funds.

THE HOME OFFICE

You'll recall that in Chapter 10 I asked that you not place your desk directly in line with the door. I further suggested you face the door, not sit with your back to it (see the illustration in that chapter). Feng shui teaches that not only do you want to see who is entering the room, there is a metaphorical meaning to the setup. You don't want people sneaking up behind you in life.

If you cannot move that desk, here are some simple cures:

◆ Hang a chime over the desk.

◆ Place an object in front of the desk as a buffer for the energy. A plant is the logical choice. If you have no luck with plants, you can use silk. Place one teaspoon of soil from a place that has significance to you in the silk plant to "activate" it. In feng shui terms it will now serve the same purpose as a living plant.

NO DRIED FLOWERS

Avoid decorating with dried flowers, which represent death in general. The exception would be if they have enormous positive sentimental significance in your life, such as your dried wedding bouquet.

◆ Hang a mirror (the octagonal shape of the bagua would be ideal) at eye level so all you need do is look up to see who is behind you.

◆ Try to have a standing light fixture or track lighting over your desk no matter what its position. This will symbolize light or wisdom on your work. You work will be illuminated in the esoteric sense.

◆ A glass desk is highly decorative but it makes thinking a little more difficult because nothing anchors the chi. Feng shui says the chi will fly through the glass. If you have a glass desk, place an elephant figurine or paperweight on your desk. Being the heaviest land mammals, they anchor the energy wherever they are placed.

THE BEDROOMS

By now you realize that plants (lucky bamboo is a classic), chimes, and mirrors are some of the most common cures in feng shui. Bamboo flutes are also popular. Work your cures into the décor so they do not call attention to themselves. Even in the absence of a problem, these cures enhance the chi.

Here is a wonderful step to take to boost the health of everyone in the home. Use it for every bed in the home.

At your local craft store, purchase the nine feng shui colors (as indicated on the bagua) in felt squares. Cut these into the bagua shape with one exception: The yellow must be a circle.

Stand at the foot of your bed. Even though no one enters here, this is the entry point from a feng shui perspective. Place the black bagua in the middle between the box spring and the mattress. We use felt so the baguas won't go flying every time you make the bed! To your left in the corner spot, place the blue bagua and work your way around the entire bed. In the center use your yellow circle.

This is especially effective if you have a sick person in the home. Wouldn't it be nice if hospital beds had baguas hidden between the box spring and the mattress!

By the way, you can also cut the colors out of construction paper and place the pattern under your desk at home and at work.

THE COMMON ROOMS

You will certainly want to introduce a few feng shui touches to these rooms. You want to make the common rooms comfortable family gathering spots. You will also be creating over time an inviting energy that makes guests feel instantly at home. We have all entered homes that made us feel like a member of the family. We have also entered homes that were stiff and uncomfortable. It isn't always the décor that speaks to us. Sometimes it's the feel of the room. Let's examine some of the things you can try:

- ◆ If you have windows with no covering, hang a crystal in the center. This cure is important for all the rooms in your home or office. I have seen a crystal in the shape of a bagua that is sold as a rainbow catcher. Something like this is ideal! The premise is that you don't want the chi flying out the window. You want to build it and invite it to stay within the family walls.

◆ Try to have a bookcase in the Skill and Knowledge section as you enter most rooms. The common rooms are frequently where we find the family collection of books. Why not place your bookcase in accordance with good feng shui? No wall space available? As I enter my kitchen, I have a treasured cookbook sitting on top of the microwave. No one knows it is a feng shui placement. You don't have to have a bookcase in every room of your house. Sometimes just one book will do the trick. Remember that feng shui uses a symbolic language.

◆ Hang certificates of higher education or awards you have earned in these areas. It seems a shame to work hard to receive them and then put them in a drawer. They can be silent motivators for your children.

THE GARAGE, ATTIC, OR STORAGE SPACE

No, I am not going to suggest you use feng shui for these spaces. I do, however, want you to be aware that every home, every storage facility, and indeed every property you own or rent, affects you. Keep these areas tidy and organized to promote your good fortune!

A FENG SHUI PERSPECTIVE

Look at your entire piece of property from a feng shui perspective. What if your messy storage shed is behind the garage in the relationships corner of the property? No one outside the family may see its contents, but do you want a hidden mess in such a powerful area?

GENEROSITY OF SPIRIT

Feng shui might not appeal to you. And yet you might still long to make your home a haven. There are numerous ways to make one's space sacred. Let us turn our attention to a few additional healing modalities.

THE AMERICAN INDIAN TRADITION

You can purchase a sage stick in most health food stores, alternative or New Age shops, and even large supermarkets. They are a wonderful and easy way to cleanse your home of unwanted negative energy. I like to do this on a weekly basis. We all have unpleasant phone conversations, the occasional argument, workmen, or even houseguests in the house. To keep the energy in the home strong and personal to its occupants, light your sage stick with a match. After about 40 seconds blow it out. You will have an aromatic plume of smoke. Wave this in the room, asking that any negativity be released. Trace the doors and windows, asking that no one enter this home who does not respect you and the values of your family.

This practice is especially important when you move into a new space. You want to release the energy left behind by the previous owners, no matter who they were or how perfect they seem.

HELP FROM THE SCIENCE OF YOGA

Most Americans view yoga as a series of pretzel-like positions. Yoga postures are far more than a form of exercise. They are actually a part of an ancient spiritual philosophy. The postures were designed to enhance the physical body's ability to handle more energy entering the body as the result of meditation.

Yogis burn incense the way American Indians burn sage in order to seal the doors and windows and clear the home. I do this practice every Friday night. In addition, I burn candles every Sunday evening to welcome the new week.

Remember, too, that in yoga the place of meditation was kept sacred for that purpose alone. Over time, the energy of the practice got strong and helped you on days when being quiet and still was especially difficult. Just so, we can take this concept and apply it to every part of our home. Do we not weaken the nurturing atmosphere of the kitchen when we turn the counters into a dumping ground for mail and homework? We can choose to honor the function of each room or we can turn the house into an upside-down mish mash of everything that takes place there. I suggest we learn from the science of yoga how powerful dedication of purpose can be.

A RESPECTFUL MENTION

In the ancient cultures of India and Japan, two additional philosophies governing the creation of the home as personal sanctuary were born. I mention them here briefly. My hope is that you will have some guidance should your quest not have been satisfied by any of the modalities I use.

From Japan we have Shibui, the philosophy referred to as "the cultivation of the little" or "the art of not too much." What we in the West often view as austerity when we see the ancient Japanese home can be viewed instead as a reverence or respect for space. I enter some of today's homes and wonder if we as a culture have not come to find our security in the accumulation of stuff. You needn't pare down to the bone the items in your home. You might simply take a clue from Shibui and find a willingness to eliminate your clutter. Organize one area and see if you are more comfortable there than in any other place in your home. You needn't accept any philosophy until you see for yourself the merits of its teachings.

India has graced us with an ancient system called Vastu. This philosophy is very much akin in approach to the Compass School of Fung Shui. In both you will find specific rules and regulations to follow in setting up the home with an eye to a higher purpose. There are books on Vastu in your local library. In addition, Vastu practitioners are growing in number. You might want to arrange a consultation. Start your quest at your local library or bookstore and begin to educate yourself on this ancient area that pre-dates feng shui!

FINAL NOTE

In the aftermath of September 11, we have become especially sensitive to the need for peace in our personal space. Nurturing environments are the natural antidotes to the chaos in the world we have experienced and over which we have no control. You and your partner should research all the possibilities and see which philosophy you feel most comfortable with for your budding sanctuary. You might even decide you are comfortable borrowing from several traditions to create a space that uniquely expresses your values and beliefs. Whatever comforts your soul is no doubt the correct answer.

RESOURCES

There are many books, websites, stores, and other resources available to help you get organized. Here are some of the ones I use and urge my students to take advantage of.

BOOKS

AROMATHERAPY

Worwood, Valerie Ann. *The Complete Book of Essential Oils & Aromatherapy.* New World Library, 1991 (ISBN 0-931432-82-0).

EMOTIONAL/PHYSICAL/PSYCHOLOGICAL SUPPORT

Bradshaw, John. *The Family: A New Way of Creating Solid Self Esteem.* Health Communications, revised 1990 (ISBN 155874274).

———. *Healing the Shame That Binds You.* Health Communications, 1988 (ISBN 0932194869).

———. *Homecoming: Reclaiming and Championing Your Inner Child.* Bantam Doubleday Del, 1992 (ISBN 0553353896).

Cameron, Julia. *The Artist's Way*. Putnam, 1992 (ISBN 0-87477-694-5).

FENG SHUI

Rossbach, Sarah. *Feng Shui: The Chinese Art of Placement*. Penguin/Arkana, 1991 (ISBN 0-14-019353-7).

————. *Interior Design with Feng Shui*. Penguin/Arkana, 1987 (ISBN 0-14-019352-9).

Kingston, Karen. *Creating Sacred Space with Feng Shui: Learn the Art of Space Clearing and Bring New Energy into Your Life*. Broadway Books, 1997 (ISBN 0553069160).

ORGANIZING

Leeds, Regina. *The Zen of Organizing: Creating Order and Peace in Your Home, Career, and Life*. Alpha Books, 2002 (ISBN 0-02-864265-1).

STORES/CATALOGS THAT CARRY ORGANIZING PRODUCTS

The Container Store
www.containerstore.com
1-800-733-3532

Hold Everything
www.holdeverything.com
1-800-421-2264

Ikea
www.ikea.com
1-800-434-4532

Bed, Bath & Beyond
www.bedbathandbeyond.com
1-800-462-3966

Lillian Vernon
www.lillianvernon.com
1-800-545-5426

OFFICE PRODUCTS

Reliable Home Office
www.reliablehomeoffice.com
1-800-869-6000

Staples
www.staples.com
1-800-3-STAPLE

Office Max
www.officemax.com
1-800-788-8080

JUNK MAIL ELIMINATION

Mail Preference Service
Direct Marketing Association
PO Box 9008
Farmingdale, NY 11735

PROFESSIONAL ORGANIZERS

Regina Leeds
Get Organized! by REGINA
www.reginaleeds.com
818-506-7167

National Association of Professional Organizers
www.NAPO.net
770-325-3440

CLOSET DESIGN

Closets by Design
www.closetsbydesign.com
1-800-293-3744

MOVERS

Stratton and Son Moving and Storage
(serving California, Nevada, and Arizona)
818-365-4393

YOGA AND MEDITATION

Yoga Center of California
445 East 17th Street
Costa Mesa, CA 92627
www.yogacenter.org or www.mysticworldfellowship.net
949-646-8281

INDEX

A

action files, 207
activity zones, kitchen,
  116-128
  baking, 122
  clean-up, 125
  cooking, 118-120
  countertops, 125-127
  food preparation,
    120-122
  food storage, 122-125
  islands, 127-128
  pantries, 122-125
  table setting, 120-122
American Indian traditions,
  creating sacred spaces, 233
appliances, kitchen,
  115-116

archive files, 205-206
attics, 190-192

B

bagua (feng shui), 221-222
baking, areas in kitchen, 122
basement organization, 162
baskets, harvest, 124
bathrooms, 134-136
  children, 145
  feng shui tips, 228-229
  guests, 145-146
  inventory, 136-138
  linen closet, 146-147
  merging homes,
    147-148

organizing, 138-139
  elimination, 139-140
  fitting all in, 141
  preparation, 139
  shelf creators, 140-141
  single categories at a
    time, 139
  special collections,
    141-144
bedrooms, 80
  closets, 89-99
  clothing, 86-89
  double-duty room,
    103-104
  dressers, 99-101
  feng shui tips, 230-231
  jewelry, 101-102
  nightstands, 83-85
  purpose, 102-103
  under-bed storage, 86
  unmade beds, 81-82
beds
  storage underneath, 86
  unmade, 81-82
bicycle storage, garage, 188
Black Hat School of Feng
  Shui, 220-221
bookcases, home offices, 212
boxes, labeling for move,
  63-66
Bradshaw, John, 9

C

cassette tape storage, family
  room, 158-159
categorizing, garage organization, 186
CD storage, family room,
  158-159
change
  past influences, 5
  resistance to, 3-5
  time control issues, 5-6
charts, children's chores, 175
children
  bathrooms, 145
  bedrooms, 169
    closets, 170-171
    furniture, 169-170
    sharing rooms, 172
    toy storage, 171-172
  chores, 168-169
    charts, 175
    distributing responsi-
      bilities, 173
    rewards, 173-175
  kitchen, 110
  toy storage
    bedrooms, 171-172
    family room storage,
      152-155

Chinese Compass School (feng shui), 221

chores
charting responsibilities, 18-23
children's, 168-169
charts, 175
distributing responsibilities, 173
rewards, 173-175

clean-up, kitchen, 125

closets
bathrooms, linen closet, 146-147
bedrooms, 89-99
children's rooms, 170-171
hall closets, 163-164
linen, 146-147
organizing, 89
clothing, 96-97
creating space, 97-99
deciding what to keep, 90-93
lines of clothing, 90
preparation, 89
shelves and floor, 93-96

clothing, 86-89
organizing, 96-97

collections, family room storage, 160

common rooms, 150
dens, 160
deciding how you want the room to function, 160
deciding what you need, 161
setting up the room, 162
family rooms, 152
family-friendly furniture, 155-157
hobbies/collections, 160
media storage, 159-160
music collection, 158-159
photos and memorabilia, 157-158
storing children's toys, 152-155
feng shui tips, 231-232
finished basements, 162
formal living rooms, 151-152
mess-free activities, 152
plants, 151
hall closets, 163-164

Complete Idiot's Guide to Smart Moving, The, 57

containers, kitchen, 123
control freaks, 53-56
cooking, kitchen, 118-120
countertops, kitchen,
    125-127
creating sacred spaces
    American Indian traditions,
        233
    feng shui, 220-232
        bagua, 221-222
        bathroom tips, 228-229
        bedroom tips, 230-231
        Black Hat School, 221
        Chinese Compass
            School, 221
        common room tips,
            231-232
        fish tanks, 225-226
        home office tips,
            229-230
        kitchen tips, 229
        unification of body,
            mind and soul,
            226-227
    Shibui, 234
    Vastu, 234
    yoga traditions, 233-234
cupboards, glass-fronted, 110
cutlery, 112

D–E

dens, 160
    deciding how you want the
        room to function, 160
    deciding what you need,
        161
    setting up the room, 162
desks, home offices, 204-205
diaries, 7-9
    garage issues, 182-183
    home office space issues,
        197
    inner child, 9
    organization goals,
        213-217
    pet ownership responsibili-
        ties, 176-177
    selection, 8
    See also journals
dishes, 109-110
double-duty rooms, 103-104
drawers, 99-101
    kitchen, 111
dressers, 99-101
DVD storage, family room,
    159-160

experiences, past influences, 5

F

Family, The, 9

family rooms, 152
  family-friendly furniture,
    155-157
  hobbies/collections, 160
  media storage, 159-160
  music collection, 158-159
  photos and memorabilia,
    157-158
  storing children's toys, 152
    enlisting children's help,
      153-155

family-friendly furniture,
  155-157

feng shui, 220-221
  bagua, 221-222
  Black Hat School, 221
  Chinese Compass School,
    221
  cures for areas of your
    home, 228-232
    bathrooms, 228-229
    bedrooms, 230-231
    common rooms,
      231-232
    home offices, 229-230
    kitchen, 229

fish tanks, 225-226
  unification of body, mind,
    and soul, 226-227

files, home offices, 205
  action, 207
  archive, 205-206
  personal, 206
  reference, 206
  systems, 207-212
  work, 206

finished basements, 162

first-aid supplies, 113

fish tanks (feng shui),
  225-226

floors, closet organization,
  93-96

food
  meal planning, 129
  preparation, area in
    kitchen, 120-122
  shopping, 129
  storage, 122-125

formal living rooms, 151-152
  mess-free activities, 152
  plants, 151

furniture
  children's rooms, 169-170
  family-friendly, 155-157

G

garage, 181
  creating a workable storage
    space, 184-186
    categorizing, 186
    elimination, 186
    organization, 187-190
    supplies for clean-up
      day, 185
  journal questions,
    182-183
  stored items, 183
garbage cans, bathroom, 143
goals, journaling organization,
  213-217
guests
  bathrooms, 145-146
  bedrooms, 178

H

habits
  establishing, 16
  past patterns, 16-18
  unmade beds, 81-82
  untidy nightstands, 83-85
hall closets, 163-164
hampers, 143
harvest baskets, 124
Healing the Shame That Binds, 9

hobbies, storing materials,
  160
holiday items
  kitchen organization,
    114-115
  ornament storage, 187
home offices, 203-204
  assessing needs, 196
  attention to detail, 203
  bookcases, 212
  desks, 204-205
  feng shui tips, 229-230
  files, 205
    action, 207
    archive, 205-206
    personal, 206
    reference, 206
    systems, 207-212
    work, 206
  journal questions, 197
  multiple-use rooms, 212
  physical space, 199
  storage of supplies,
    201-203
  study in sharing office
    space, 198-199
Homecoming, 9
homes
  chores, charting responsi-
    bilities, 18-23

merging, 13-16
  bathrooms, 147-148
  kitchen, 130-132
  moving possessions,
    66-72
  personality types,
    39-56
  possession inventories,
    36-39
  second marriages, 35
  sanctuary, 11-13
hooks, bathroom, 143

I

inner child, journaling, 9
inventories
  bathrooms, 136-138
  possessions, 25-30
islands, kitchen, 127-128

J

jewelry, 101-102
journals, 7-9
  garage issues, 182-183
  home office space issues,
    197
  inner child, 9
  moving, 72-73
  organization goals, 213-217

pet ownership responsibilities, 176-177
selection of, 8
See also diaries

K

kitchen, 106-108
  activity zones, 116-117
    baking, 122
    clean-up, 125
    cooking, 118-120
    countertops, 125-127
    food preparation,
      120-122
    food storage, 122-125
    islands, 127-128
    pantries, 122-125
    table setting, 120-122
  creating inviting spaces,
    132
  feng shui tips, 229
  large appliances, 115-116
  laundry rooms, 130
  meal planning, 129
  merging homes, 130-132
  organizing, 108-109
    children, 110
    dishes, 109-110
    drawers, 111

glass-fronted cupboards, 110
holiday items, 114-115
refrigerators, 113-114
shelf liners, 112
silverware, 112
spices, 112-113
tools and first-aid supplies, 113
underneath sinks, 128-129

L

labeling boxes, 63-66
laundry hampers, 143
laundry rooms, 130
linen closets, 146-148

M

magazines, 84
makeup storage, bathrooms, 142
marriages, second, 35
media storage, family room, 159-160
medication storage, bathroom, 144
memorabilia storage, family room, 157-158

merging homes, 13-16
bathrooms, 147-148
kitchens, 130-132
moving possessions, 66-67
deciding what to keep, 67-68
emotional attachments, 70-72
making space, 68-70
personality types, 39-40
packrats, 40-43
past lessons, 52-56
perfectionists, 47-52
procrastinators, 47-52
sentimental savers, 44-47
possession inventories, 36-39
second marriages, 35
mess-free activities, formal living room, 152
movers
selection, 58-63
unpacking possessions, 61
moving
day of, 73-75
journals, 72-73
merging possessions, 66-67

deciding what to keep, 67-68

emotional attachments, 70-72

making space, 68-70

one room at a time, 76-77

preparation, 63-66

selecting a mover, 58-63

supply checklist, 76

multiple-use rooms, 212

music storage, family room, 158-159

N–O

natural disaster preparedness, garage organization, 190

nightstands, 83-85

off-site storage, 192-193

organization

attics, 190-192

bathrooms, 138-139

elimination, 139-140

fitting all in, 141

preparation, 139

shelf creators, 140-141

single categories at a time, 139

bedroom closets, 89

clothing, 96-97

creating space, 97-99

deciding what to keep, 90-93

lines of clothing, 90

preparation, 89

shelves and floor, 93-96

children's rooms, 169

closets, 170-171

furniture, 169-170

sharing rooms, 172

toy storage, 171-172

dens, 160

deciding how you want the room to function, 160

deciding what you need, 161

setting up the room, 162

family rooms, 152

family-friendly furniture, 155-157

hobbies/collections, 160

media storage, 159-160

music collection, 158-159

photos and memorabilia, 157-158

storing children's toys, 152-155

finished basements, 162
formal living rooms, 151
  mess-free activities, 152
  plants, 151
garage, 181-190
  bicycle storage, 188
  creating a workable storage space, 184-186
  holiday ornaments, 187
  journal questions, 182-183
  natural disaster preparedness, 190
  shelf space, 190
  sports equipment, 188
  stored items, 183
  tools, 189
guest rooms, 178
hall closets, 163-164
home offices, 203-204
  assessing needs, 196
  attention to detail, 203
  bookcases, 212
  desks, 204-205
  files, 205-212
  journal questions, 197
  physical space, 199
  storage of supplies, 201-203
  study in sharing office space, 198-199

journaling goals, 213-217
kitchens, 108-109
  children, 110
  dishes, 109-110
  drawers, 111
  glass-fronted cupboards, 110
  holiday items, 114-115
  refrigerators, 113-114
  shelf liners, 112
  silverware, 112
  spices, 112-113
  tools and first-aid supplies, 113
overzealous organizers, 193
possessions, 30-31
  past influences, 33-35
  second marriages, 35
  three-step formula, 31-33
outside storage, 184
overzealous organizers, 193

P–Q

packrats, 40-43
pantries, 122-125
perfectionists, 47-52
personal files, 206

personality types, 39-40
  control freaks, 52-56
  packrats, 40-43
  perfectionists, 47-52
  procrastinators, 47-52
  sentimental savers, 44-47
pet ownership, 176-178
photo storage, family room,
  157-158
physical space, home offices,
  199
placement, feng shui,
  220-232
  bagua, 221-222
  bathrooms, 228-229
  bedrooms, 230-231
  Black Hat School, 221
  Chinese Compass School,
    221
  common rooms, 231-232
  fish tanks, 225-226
  home offices, 229-230
  kitchen, 229
  unification of body, mind,
    and soul, 226-227
planning, 166-167
plants, formal living room, 151
possessions, 24-25
  merging homes, 66-67
    deciding what to keep,
      67-68

emotional attachments,
  70-72
inventories, 36-39
making space, 68-70
organizing, 30-31
  past influences, 33-35
  second marriages, 35
  three-step formula,
    31-33
personality types, 39-40
  packrats, 40-43
  past lessons, 52-56
  perfectionists, 47-52
  procrastinators, 47-52
  sentimental savers, 44-47
taking inventory, 25-30
unpacking, 61
procrastinators, 47-52
public storage, 71-72

R

reading material, bathrooms,
  143
records (music) storage,
  family room, 158-159
reference files, 206
refrigerators, organization,
  113-114
resistance to change, 3-5
rewards, children and chores,
  173-175

S

sacred spaces
American Indian traditions,
233
feng shui, 220-232
bagua, 221-222
bathrooms, 228-229
bedrooms, 230-231
Black Hat School, 221
Chinese Compass
School, 221
common rooms,
231-232
fish tanks, 225-226
home offices, 229-230
kitchen, 229
unification of body,
mind, and soul,
226-227
Shibui, 234
Vastu, 234
yoga traditions, 233-234
sanctuaries, homes, 11-13
scheduling, 166-167
second marriages, 35
sentimental savers, 44-47
sharing rooms, children's
rooms, 172

shelves
closet organization, 93-96
creators
bathrooms, 140-141
kitchen, 124
garage organization, 190
liners, 112
Shibui, creating sacred spaces,
234
shopping for food, 129
silverware, 112
sinks
bathrooms, 142
kitchen, 128-129
spices, organizing, 112-113
sports equipment, garage
storage, 188
storage
bathrooms, 143
food, 122-125
garage, 183-190
bicycles, 188
creating a workable stor-
age space, 184-186
holiday ornaments, 187
natural disaster pre-
paredness, 190
shelf space, 190
sports equipment, 188
tools, 189

home office supplies, 201-203
off-site, 192-193
outside, 184
toys
    children's rooms, 171-172
    family rooms, 152-155
under-bed, 86
units, 71-72
stuff
    merging homes, 66-67
    deciding what to keep,
      67-68
    emotional attachments,
      70-72
    inventories, 36-39
    making space, 68-70
    organizing, 30-31
    past influences, 33-35
    second marriages, 35
    three-step formula, 31-33
    personality types, 39-40
    packrats, 40-43
    past lessons, 52-56
    perfectionists, 47-52
    procrastinators, 47-52
    sentimental savers, 44-47
    taking inventory, 25-30
    unpacking, 61
supplies, moving day, 76

T

table settings, kitchen,
  120-122
three-step formula for
  organization, 31-33
tools
  garage storage, 189
  kitchen, 113
toy storage
  children's rooms, 171-172
  family room, 152-155

U-V

unification of body, mind,
  and soul, feng shui,
  226-227
unpacking possessions,
  movers, 61

Vastu, creating sacred spaces,
  234
VHS tape storage, family
  rooms, 159-160
video game storage, family
  rooms, 159-160

W–X

work files, 206
workable storage space
  (garage), 184-187
    bicycle storage, 188
    categorizing, 186
    elimination, 186
    holiday ornament storage,
      187
    natural disaster prepared-
      ness, 190
    shelf space, 190
    sports equipment, 188
    supplies for clean-up day,
      185
    tools, 189

Y–Z

yoga traditions, creating
  sacred spaces, 233-234

*Zen of Organizing: Creating
  Order and Peace in Your
  Home, Career, and Life, The,*
  10

ABOUT THE AUTHOR

Regina Leeds has been featured in national magazines, including *Bon Appetit, Redbook,* Delta Airlines' *Shuttle Sheet, The Utne Reader,* and *New Age Magazine.* She is a resident expert at the Home and Garden Channel at iVillage.com. Regina is currently developing a TV series for the Fine Living Cable Channel with Emmy Award–winning producer George Merlis of Fisher/Merlis Television.

A New York City native, Regina has brought order to home and work environments across the United States since 1988, when she started her company, Get Organized! by Regina. Currently based in Los Angeles, her clientele runs the gamut from studio executives and artists to businesspeople and housewives. Regina regularly travels throughout the United States to assist her clients.

Raised a Roman Catholic in Brooklyn, Regina later studied religious science for more than 10 years. Following the path of founder Ernest Holmes, she studied the spiritual philosophies of the East. This serendipitously dovetailed with her work as a professional organizer and led to the birth of "Zen Organizing." Regina has taught classes and delivered speeches on the art of Zen Organizing to diverse groups around the country. In the fall of 2000, Regina self-published her first book, *The Zen of Organizing: Creating Order and Peace in Your Home, Career, and Life,* which was later published by Alpha Books.

Regina's first career as a professional actress (she received a Bachelor's degree in theater from Hunter College in Manhattan) has made the transition to teacher and seminar leader an easy one. Regina's credits as a professional actress include national commercials, guest spots on TV, theater roles, and three happy years recurring on *The Young and the Restless.*

Her Golden Retriever, Miss Katie, and her ever-cranky cockatiel, Murphy, thank you for your interest in their human mother's career.